GOETHE REVISITED

*Lectures delivered in sundry places
and on various dates to mark the 150th
anniversary of Goethe's death.*

This volume is published simultaneously as Volume 30 in the Series Publications of the Institute of Germanic Studies (University of London) and in collaboration with the Goethe-Institut, London.

Oil Portrait of Goethe by J.K. Stieler, taken from *On Wings of Song: A Biography of Felix Mendelssohn* by Wilfrid Blunt. Courtesy of Robert Harding Picture Library.

GOETHE REVISITED
A Collection of Essays

Edited by Elizabeth M. Wilkinson

John Calder · London
Riverrun Press · New York

First published in Great Britain 1984 by
John Calder (Publishers) Ltd.,
18 Brewer Street,
London W1R 4AS

and first published in the USA 1983 by
Riverrun Press Inc.,
175 Fifth Avenue,
New York, NY 10010

SUBSIDISED BY THE
Arts Council
OF GREAT BRITAIN

British Library Cataloguing in Publication Data

Goethe revisted: a collection of essays
   1. Goethe, Johann Wolfgang von — Criticism and Interpretation
   I. Wilkinson, Elizabeth M.
   831'.6   PT 1904
ISBN 0 7145 3951 1 paperback
ISBN 0 85457 110 8 (Institute of Germanic Studies)

Photoset in 10/12pt Baskerville by Margaret Spooner Typesetting, Dorset

Printed and bound by The Guernsey Press Company Ltd.

CONTENTS

ABBREVIATIONS

The essays in this volume refer to Goethe's works by using the following abbreviations:

HA *Goethes Werke.* Hamburger Ausgabe, ed. Erich Trunz et al., 14 vols, Hamburg, Wegner, 1948-60
Goethes Briefe. Hamburger Ausgabe, ed. Karl Robert Mandelkow and Bodo Morawe, 4 vols, Hamburg, Wegner, 1962-67

WA *Goethes Werke.* Weimarer Ausgabe, Weimar, Böhlau, 1887-1919. Part I, 55 vols; Part II: Naturwissenschaftliche Schriften, 13 vols; Part III: Tagebücher, 15 vols; Part IV: Briefe, 50 vols

GA *Gedenkausgabe der Werke, Briefe und Gespräche*, ed. Ernst Beutler, 24 + 2 supplementary vols, Zurich, Artemis, 1948-64

A glance at the individual titles will show that this collection
makes no pretence to a well-conducted tour around Goethe's
manifold achievements. Something on those lines was apparently
in the mind of planners and publishers. It had to be abandoned;
not primarily because several of that ilk are available and others
promised — plurality, if not of our present chaotic sort, is of the
essence of scholarship — but because of practicalities implicit in
the original idea. This was one of several floated by a committee
convened to co-ordinate plans for commemorating the 150th
anniversary of his death on 22 March 1982. Nothing so grandiose,
or sorely needed, as the twelve-volume translation of his selected
works launched concurrently with a 'Goethe Society of North
America' a couple of years ago. Though under the presidency of
Victor Lange of Princeton this is California based; unlike the older
one which, inspired from Wisconsin in its better days, was by the
time I knew it in the 'fifties run from the Johns Hopkins
University, and very much part of the 'Eastern Seabord Establishment'. A not uninteresting shift in geo-cultural perspectives! But
in more modest vein the English Goethe Society offered a prize
for the translation of Goethe poems (and had a surprising
number of entries); the BBC a series of talks and a production of
both parts of *Faust*; the Institute of Germanic Studies an exhibition
of 'Faust on the German Stage'. While the Goethe-Institut
undertook the organization and funding of a much more ambitious
project: an exhibition illustrating his life and work, which after
opening in London would tour other centres — accompanied at
each station by a lecture destined for a commemorative volume.

I had preferred not to be involved this time round, having done
more than my bit for Goethe during the bicentenary of his birth in
1949. Definitely not the right ground to have chosen! Would I not,
precisely because of that previous experience, consider coming
out of reclusive retirement at least far enough to edit this volume
— and invite the speakers? It didn't need benefit of hindsight to see
snags in this, on the face of it not unattractive, idea: if local interest

was to be assured, university terms would have to be considered; if publication was to be achieved within the year, some lecturers would have to submit their mss for editing well before delivering their lecture; some centres, while welcoming the exhibition, might be intent on recruiting speakers from local talent. After a number of false starts resulting in offerings clearly designed for a quite different occasion, or no occasion at all, and of interest to none but Germanists, I decided on a different tack. I would approach scholars who had said or written something which stuck in my mind not only for its intrinsic interest but as indicative of unfinished business, and see what happened. And I would not feel bound by tiresomely unfeasible links with the exhibition! So that in the event only three of the following coincided with it; and only six were delivered at a Goethe-Institut. R.H. Stephenson's and T.J. Reed's were both arranged for commemorative occasions elsewhere: the former at Glasgow University last March; the latter at a Joint Conference of University Teachers of German and the English Goethe Society held at Queen Mary College in early April. My own piece was never intended to be published here, or — in its present form — anywhere else. It was a broadcast (also unintended!) which went out on the anniversary itself under the title 'Goethe and Love': despite the best efforts of my producer the *Radio Times* wouldn't wear its original, far more precise name even as sub-title. But when two of my speakers were prevented from delivering a text for press I was persuaded to put it in. Not least by many confiding letters from total strangers. Only one 'Disgusted, Tunbridge Wells'. And had this tended to deter me in my declining years I had only to recall quite different reactions from the National Institute of Mental Health, Washington DC. Having obtained a tape of its first public performance at Smith College in 1966, they were enthusiastically relaying it in their programmes on sex education.

There were only two conditions I imposed on my eventual contributors: no lectures confined to discussion of a single work; and nothing, *p-lease*, of the 'Goethe und . . .' variety. They were all very good about both. Even the two who did opt for this form of title were obviously going to assign to the copula a connective function far from flabby. 'Goethe and the lied' eschews that potage of anecdote, opinion and 'taste' familiar from so much babble on 'Goethe und die Musik' in favour of a trenchant explanation of his disconcerting preference for inferior settings of his own poems and our, even more disconcerting, penchant for superb settings of the trivial or the trite. While 'Goethe and Happiness' invites us to inspect the proposition that this was not only a quality of life for which he had a natural talent but a traditional value he increasingly espoused as a mission: to provide exemplars which may sustain us amid the unavoidable tribulations of this mortal life, and thereby serve as counter-models in a culture bent on the celebration of pain for its own sake, and its gratuitous elevation to the status of tragedy. They thus adopt an argumentative stance shared in greater or lesser degree by all the contributors. A case is defended; should we wish to dispute or emend it, we at least know where to take off from. Unforeseen, and certainly unplanned, a unifying trend had emerged in these disparate revisitings. A trend subversive, not of Goethe himself, but of stock images which persist because they are self-propagating. Iconoclastic therefore. But in favour of what? Scarcely of the 'whole' Goethe. Though he himself left us an unambiguous pointer to the unifying principle of his many-facetted existence, we still seem aeons away from cottoning on to it in our private or our public life. And in our present parlous-seeming predicament Carlyle's guesstimate that it would take more than a thousand years may in the event prove either irrelevantly naive or quite unnecessarily long. What we have here is just something worth our present while to be going on with: the image of a practical, down-to-earth realist, in philosophy as in life; a human, often all-too-human, being.

There are a few signs, not enough, as this anniversary year draws to its close, that some chipping away at graven images may be taking place in fringe activities. Premiere productions of *Faust* in a translation by the American poet, Randall Jarrell, are announced at the Cockpit Theatre for December (Part One) and next January (Part Two), and may lead us to infer some understandable dissatisfaction with the MacNeice/Stahl version used by the BBC. A recent production of *Torquato Tasso* at the Citizens' Theatre in Glasgow must finally have put paid to the legend, fostered by the charismatic presence of Josef Kainz in the echoing vastnesses of the Wiener Burgtheater, that this is a character study of the wayward poet. And one review of R.D. MacDonald's highly personal translation by Ned Chaillet in *The Times* on 30 October 1982 lifted my heart by its exact appreciation of the movement and texture of Goethe's own verse: '[his] German laps forward syllable by syllable, each word retaining echoes of preceding words . . .'. Would that I could, as BBC consultant in 1949, have persuaded translator or producer that this is also true of *Egmont*: that its prose is already aspiring to the condition of verse; that the structure of its encounter-scenes, not least the use of stichomythia, points forward to Goethe's classical plays, to chamber-theatre — and away from Shakespeare. We might then have been spared the sort of self-justification permitted in the 'Londoner's Diary' of *The Standard* for 22 October 1982. Under a notice of 'The first London performance of a work by Beethoven' we were offered the overture and complete incidental music, boiled down to some twenty minutes on the grounds that the play 'does not rise very far above mediocrity': the hero is 'not very virile, and slow to anger . . . he even sees some point to what the Spanish are saying.' Maybe the adapter should read more of *The Observer*; and *much* more of *Cosmopolitan*; though I doubt Beethoven would have needed this sort of support in order to disagree with him. Cutting is a fine art. And one which may be approached from two distinguishable points of view: that of form and style; or that of the import these embody. It was because this latter had been so marvellously grasped by that great educator, Arnold Freeman, that his production of the whole of *Faust*, on a single evening, by members of his Sheffield Educational Settlement at the Rudolf Steiner Hall in London, remains by far the most vivid impression I retain of all the many activities of the 1949 celebrations. But there are some quaint things one would not gladly forgo when one is, as I have been in various capacities for forty years, at the receiving end of enquiries. Yes, they have increased. Yes, he is more often quoted — and for the most part more accurately. But who'd be without the mirth of 'Blind Cow' as the title of one of Goethe's rococo poems, announced by a distinguished musician on the highbrow Radio 3? When I was a little girl we used to call that party game 'Blind Man's Buff'. All things considered however, I'll wager — though not a betting man — that we won't have this year, or for some time to come, anything approaching a leader in the *Evening Standard* of 25 February 1936, on the Jubilee of the English Goethe Society:

> Goethe is no longer included, as he once was, among the little group of world geniuses . . . his life counts against him heavily. He was a snob of the most obvious sort, who treasured a handkerchief into which Napoleon had blown his nose, and kept his mistress in the kitchen because of her bad table manners.

A Perilous Multiplicity   Michael Hamburger

Goethe's place in world literature — as representative man, great European, and universal sage — has long been secure. The foundations for it were laid even in his own lifetime. Yet one cannot help being struck by a disparity between such generally acknowledged status and the extent to which his works are actually read and appreciated outside the German-speaking world — or outside the German Departments of universities. It was that disparity, misunderstood and misinterpreted, which could allow T.S. Eliot to declare in 1933 that 'of Goethe perhaps it is truer to say that he dabbled both in philosophy and poetry and made no great success of either; his true role was that of the man of the world and sage, a La Rochefoucauld, a La Bruyère, a Vauvenargues'.

In his Hamburg lecture of 1955, 'Goethe as the Sage', T.S. Eliot was to retract and correct this statement. Since Eliot himself was a poet-critic of European stature, with immense authority and influence among generations of readers in English-speaking countries and beyond, it is worth looking a little more closely at this later pronouncement on Goethe, and its bearing on the above disparity, which remains as glaringly evident today as it was in 1933 or 1955. Eliot's address was included in his 1957 collection of essays *On Poetry and Poets*; and my remarks here will also be mainly concerned with Goethe as poet, though not exclusively as a lyric poet. Since my knowledge of the reception of Goethe's work is far from being world-wide, I shall make no attempt to stray too far beyond the bounds of my limited competence as critic and my experience as translator of a few of Goethe's many works into English. Whether the disparity that was my starting-point is as marked in other European and non-European countries as it is in Britain will have to remain an open question.

T.S. Eliot's retraction of his earlier dismissal of Goethe hinges on a redefinition of the poet as sage, and on Eliot's recognition that Goethe's wisdom was not merely worldly —like that of the three French aphorists mentioned above — but spiritual. Yet the title of his later piece remained, all the same, 'Goethe as the Sage'. And though it touches on *Faust*; on the conversations with Eckermann; and even on Goethe's scientific writings, not a single poem of Goethe's is quoted or so much as referred to in the address. Goethe's excellence as a lyric poet is assumed — but never exemplified; and it is assumed on the grounds that Goethe was something more than, and other than, a mere poet:

> Poetic inspiration is none too common, but the true sage is rarer than the true poet; and when the two gifts, that of wisdom and that of poetic speech, are found in the same man, you have the great poet. It is poets of that kind who belong, not merely to their own people but to the world; it is only poets of this kind of whom one can think, not primarily as limited by their own language and nation, but as great Europeans.

On these grounds Eliot promoted Goethe from the company of La Rochefoucauld, La Bruyère and Vauvenargues to that of Dante and Shakespeare — poets whose entire work remains of exemplary importance to every educated European — as distinct from Cervantes, the author of a single masterpiece of the same order. Yet, once more, of Goethe's poetic and dramatic works only *Faust* is mentioned by Eliot. Judging by the availability of English translations — that is, by the demand for English versions of Goethe's work — it would seem that Goethe's place in the awareness of English-speaking readers is in fact more like that of Cervantes than that of Dante or Shakespeare. *Faust* has been translated again and again. Translations of other works by Goethe do appear from time to time; but without receiving comparable attention, or establishing themselves as standard versions, like the Schlegel-Tieck versions of Shakespeare or Cary's Dante. There is no indication in T.S. Eliot's lecture that he knew and appreciated any imaginative work of Goethe's other than *Faust*. And this in a lecture that makes a claim for the importance of Goethe's entire work for English-speaking and European readers. Significantly enough, Eckermann's conversations with Goethe *are* mentioned in the lecture; and Eliot has something to say about the degree to which Goethe's person, opinions and activities have gone on being documented ever since his lifetime, whereas we know so little about Dante's, and even less about Shakespeare's. I shall have to return to this crucial difference.

As for Eliot's earlier statement about Goethe — which could well have been based on a reading of Eckermann's conversations alone — he attributes it partly to ignorance, partly to an antipathy rooted in differences of outlook and temperament, partly to a general prejudice against poets of the Romantic period. What is striking here is that Eliot seemed unaware, even in 1955, of Goethe's own rejection of all that he felt to be morbid and one-sided in the Romantic movement; of Goethe's deliberate classicism, or classicizing, in one phase of his long productive life; and of the degree to which much of Goethe's work is either pre-Romantic or post-Romantic. This points to one of the major obstacles to an understanding and appreciation of Goethe's work as a whole outside German-speaking countries. Goethe did indeed have something in common with the English poets of his time: from Burns and Scott to Wordsworth and Coleridge; from Blake and Crabbe to Landor and Byron; and even to the Fitzgerald of the *Rubayat*. But not only did he cut through their specializations, incorporating something of each of them into an incomparably richer body of work; as a German writer he also took on a task that Eliot could have understood, though it remains a perplexing anachronism for the majority of British and North American readers.

Internationally speaking, Goethe was a belated 'classic' and a belated classicist — who adapted tragedies by Voltaire for the German stage long after his own so-called 'Sturm und Drang'! To English readers Goethe may look like a Romantic poet, simply because most of his work falls into their own Romantic period. What German literary historians call Goethe's 'classicism' was paradoxical in being less given than made. Made out of the need to fill gaps in German literature which only he could fill; or only he in collaboration with Schiller. Goethe's historical predicament, though, was in fact akin to that of Eliot himself, and of Ezra Pound — with their prescriptions of how and what to read, and their oppressive awareness of a literary *musée imaginaire*: a notion anticipated by Goethe's 'Weltliteratur'. It is Goethe's incomparable achievement to have imposed the unity of dominant concerns on a body of work necessarily heterogeneous in style and form, because his *musée imaginaire* called for specimens of so many different types of art that were missing from it in German; and because he had to create those specimens in conditions other than those in which the prototypes had originated and flourished. German literary historians, therefore, have had to split up their Goethe into a succession of writers: the Rococo Goethe of the early lyrics; the 'Sturm und Drang' Goethe who emulated folk-song and popular ballads, as well as Shakespeare in his dramatic works; the classicizing Goethe who emulated Euripides and Propertius and Martial; the orientalizing Goethe of the *West-östlicher Divan* — to mention only a few of them. Though of course the phases overlapped, and his 'unifying personality' (unifying 'concerns' seems more apt to me in Goethe's case) was the indispensable, and altogether modern, Ariadne's thread in the labyrinth to which his historical situation condemned him.

As Hofmannsthal knew — out of a related predicament, and a related concern with literature as cultural paradigm and institution — Goethe was both one writer and a whole literature. 'Wir haben keine neuere Literatur', Hofmannsthal wrote in his *Buch der Freunde*. 'Wir haben Goethe und Ansätze' (We have no modern literature. All we have is Goethe and beginnings'). The totality of Goethe's work —even if this were available to English-speaking readers with little or no German, which it is not — could be understood and appreciated only in the light of that anachronism, which is also a synchronism. Even if it were understood, a good many of Goethe's works — including maybe, even his *Iphigenie,* and certainly his *Natürliche Tochter* — would remain anachronisms to the ears of English-speaking readers and audiences for reasons that have to do with the medium of blank verse: a classicizing medium for Goethe and Schiller long after it had become a *live* medium for Shakespeare and his contemporaries.

Goethe's *Torquato Tasso* is usually included among his 'classical' works for that very reason: as a blank-verse tragedy related thereby to his *Iphigenie auf Tauris,* and written in the same classicizing phase. Yet thematically *Tasso* is a non-classical work — if only because classical, and even neo-classical, canons did not permit a poet to be the protagonist of a tragedy. Except in his mythical, his Orphic role, the poet as hero, as 'representative man', is a creation of the Romantic era. *Torquato Tasso* has, therefore, been interpreted mainly in terms of Goethe's biography — in contravention, once more, of classical criteria. Goethe's true classicism, I would suggest, has very little to do with his successive periods, phases and programmes. It is a quality of all his work, or of none; and it is a unique phenomenon, not to be grasped in terms of general notions of what is and is not classical.

At their most Shakespearean, Goethe and Schiller wrote their plays in prose — a prose more rhythmically and metaphorically expressive than their later blank verse. That anomaly, and Goethe's later practice of recasting dramatic prose into blank verse, points to the limitations of a too deliberate, a too anachronistic classicism, as distinct from the 'Pindaric', the rhapsodic free verse of Goethe's earlier lyric poems and dramatic fragments. That may well be one reason why *Faust* remains the only verse play of Goethe's that can be said to have established itself internationally on the stage. Another, of course, is that *Faust* comprehends all those successive Goethes. All his phases: from the Gothic to the Hellenizing and the Modern; almost all the many verse-forms that he mastered from his youth to his old age; the whole incomparable range of his interests, sympathies and wisdom.

Goethe *was* classical, though, in apportioning his individuality according to the demands of a specific *genre* or mode; and in his readiness, much of the time, to subordinate the need for self-expression to these demands. A very considerable part of his dramatic and poetic output was occasional. Not in the post-classical sense of being the response to an immediate inner experience; but in the classical sense of being produced for an outward occasion, to meet specific requirements. Amongst other things, Goethe was that very classical phenomenon: a court poet and dramatist providing entertainments generically very close to the masques of the Elizabethan age. It is Goethe scholarship of the Romantic era that shifted the emphasis entirely from this classical function of Goethe's work to his own personal development and the inward occasions. I remember having Goethe's poems presented to me at school and university exclusively in terms of his biographical circumstances or state of mind at the time of writing —usually with references to whatever girl or woman is supposed to have preoccupied him at that juncture. The tension between inner needs and outer occasions —between literature as 'fragments of a great confession' and literature as workmanship with a social or ethical function —is one of the keys to Goethe's uniqueness, as well as to the almost overwhelming diversity of his work. In his poems alone, extreme formality and extreme informality mark the two poles of the tension; and the field between them is so wide that there can be few readers capable of responding to every kind of poem he wrote. Much the same is true of his dramatic work and prose fiction.

In his 1955 address Eliot touched on this multiplicity when he observed: 'It is not easy to detect the unity in Goethe's work. For one thing, it is more bewilderingly miscellaneous than that of either of the two other men' —meaning Dante and Shakespeare. The multiplicity may have been a boon to Goethe scholars and specialists, who for the most part have only succeeded in reducing it to unity in biographical terms. But it has been as much an obstacle to appreciation of many single works by Goethe —let alone his entire *opus*, which cannot be familiar to more than a small minority of readers even in German-speaking countries — as the anachronism and paradox of his classicism. As late as 1953, in his Notes to volume IV of the Hamburg edition of Goethe's *Works,* Wolfgang Kayser felt it necessary to apologize for the fact that Goethe's robust and theatrically effective comedy *Die Mitschuldigen* is 'un-Goethean' because it cannot be related to what is known about Goethe's experiences and preoccupations at the time of writing. As though Goethe had taken a solemn vow to provide his interpreters with such data in every case! And as though it mattered! If Goethe was a truly classical, as distinct from a classicizing, writer — and he was — what matters is whether any single work stands up in its own right, true to its own laws and kind. If it does, then the unifying personality will be there, regardless of whether it is biographically documented or not; and if we look for Goethe's classicism, not in his adaptation of this or that model, or this or that verse-form, but in his irrepressible mastery of the vernacular, then *Die Mitschuldigen* needs no apology.

It is the Romantic era, beginning with Rousseau, that made the artist more interesting, more important, than the work. Ever since then, the unsigned picture has been less valuable than the signed if the attribution could not be authenticated, or if idiosyncracy did not place the provenance beyond doubt. Ever since then, too, specialization in the arts has been valued more than the breadth and scope that distinguished Goethe from all his contemporaries. Quite apart from his scientific, historical and philosophic interests, Goethe tried his hand at very nearly every existing literary *genre*: from the largest to the smallest; from verse epic, novel and tragedy to the shortest lyric, aphorism or epigram. He himself may have seemed to authorize the biographical approach to his works by stating — within the context of an autobiography — that they were 'fragments of a great confession'. From an autobiographical point of view, so are the works of any artist. In his youth especially, but throughout his life too, Goethe was uncommonly aware of being blessed with genius; but genius is a spirit, a daemon, not to be identified with personality or the ego. Even in his early celebrations of that genius it is not himself, but the power within himself and outside himself, that Goethe glorified. In later life he became more and more conscious of how much of this power was due to heredity, tradition, circumstance, and what the psychologist Groddeck was to call the 'it' or the 'id' — after immersing himself in the writings of Goethe. If that seems far-fetched one of Goethe's *Sprüche* shows that it is not:

Ihr sucht die Menschen zu benennen
Und glaubt, am Namen sie zu kennen.
Wer tiefer sieht, gesteht sich frei,
Es ist was Anonymes dabei.

One instance of Goethe's celebration of the 'id' at all periods of his life is his total freedom from shame, self-consciousness or prudery in sexual matters: from his defence of unmarried mothers in the early poem 'Vor Gericht' to the unpublishable parts of his *Roman Elegies* or *Erotica Romana*; his chronicle of sexual impotence in the poem 'Das Tagebuch', the homo-erotic allusions in *Faust* or the *West-östlicher Divan*; or, for that matter, in his 'Metamorphose der Pflanzen', with its celebration of fertility on levels rising from the biological to the ethical and the spiritual.

This brought him up against, not only the sexual morality of his

own age, but the prejudices of much later poets and critics such as
T.S. Eliot, who adduced his own puritanical antecedents in
explaining his early antagonism to Goethe. Well over a century
after Goethe's death, in 1940,[1] one of his most aesthetically
sensitive interpreters, Emil Staiger, responded with astonishment
to the poem 'Sommernacht' in the *West-östlicher Divan*, a post-
classical work that is closer in spirit to the Byzantium of W.B.
Yeats's old age than to the mild hedonism of Fitzgerald's
Victorian Persia. As Staiger noticed, in that poem the freedom in
erotic matters is matched by one in prosody, syntax and structure:
quite contrary, that is to say, to the rules laid down by Goethe
himself in his classicizing years. Yet something of that freedom is
to be found even in the *Roman Elegies*, written at the height of that
classicizing phase: in those passages where Goethe's genius of the
vernacular, of the demotic, breaks through the decorum, dignity
and exemplariness of the dominant mode — ancient Rome and
erotic love as educational paradigms. It is there, once more, that
Goethe's classicizing becomes truly classical: most akin, that is, to
the work of the ancient poets he emulated, rather than to those
plaster casts of ancient statuary that were inflicted on generations
of art students to preserve them from the taint of living, i.e. of less
than ideal, models. At its most dignified and regular, as in *Die
Natürliche Tochter,* Goethe's blank verse could turn his characters
into something chillingly reminiscent of those plaster casts.

As Staiger observed, that aspect of Goethe's classicizing is less
obtrusive in his lyric poetry than in other works of his middle and
later years. What has prevented Goethe's lyric poems from being
more accessible and familiar than they are to the English-
speaking world — including even writers and poets not in
principle averse to foreign literatures, as several prominent ones
now pride themselves on being —is due to factors as complex and
multiple as that body of his work itself. For reasons already
touched upon, the very diversity of Goethe's modes and phases is
an obstacle in itself. Those German-language poets who have to
some extent been assimilated in this century — Hölderlin and
Rilke above all — have a narrower intensity, a more evident
consistency and specialization, than Goethe as poet ever had. In
this connection it is relevant to point out that Hofmannsthal's
work, too, has failed to penetrate into anything that could be
called a general awareness in the English-speaking world —

except through the medium of music, which has done precisely the same for some of Goethe's poems and even for *Faust*. And in any partnership between music and words, music is so dominant as to virtually absorb the literary text. One other poet, Bertolt Brecht, may have broken the translation barrier; though Brecht was more like Goethe or Hofmannsthal in the range and variety of his work, and in his consciousness of its cultural and social function, than either Hölderlin or Rilke. But relative translatability and topical relevance have a good deal to do with that exception.

Translatability has been the major obstacle with those poems of Goethe's whose directness and plainness have made them an almost anonymous constituent of German popular culture. It is in the nature of such poems — songs and ballads, above all — to have their counterparts in other cultures, but to resist anything like literal translation, as distinct from imitation, especially where counterparts already exist; and there is no lack of songs and ballads in English. It is works that have no counterparts in other literatures that call for translation — another reason why *Faust*, alone among Goethe's works, is translated again and again, and, incidentally, why Brecht's poems have proved the exception they are. For as a political poet, as in his mastery of vernacular directness and plainness, Brecht has no counterpart in the English poetry of his time. Needless to say, such songs as 'Mailied' or 'Über allen Gipfeln', or the Mignon and Harpist songs from *Wilhelm Meisters Lehrjahre,* have no exact parallels in the English literature of any period, and they have uniquely Goethean qualities of subtlety and delicacy combined with plainness of diction that one would dearly like to be able to render. I have tried repeatedly to translate those poems. But though I have produced versions of some of them, I do not expect any of my versions to be more than pointers to the originals, as most versions by my many predecessors have remained. Curiously enough, the only version by me of a Goethe song that has found its way into a general anthology is of his 'Sizilianisches Lied', itself an adaptation of an Italian text by a minor poet that is omitted from some editions of Goethe's poems on those grounds! The plainer and less idiosyncratic the diction of a song-like poem, the harder it is to translate, because so much of the poem's distinction will lie not in its intellectual and intelligible substance, but in an unrepeatable concordance of sense, rhythm and sound. The response of a late

comer to the disconcerting plainness and untranslatability of
Goethe's poetry was vividly evoked by the editor of this Volume in
her Bicentenary lecture of 1949.[2] She there pointed out how
much weight of meaning is carried by even the slightest nuance —
by the initial consonants of the rhymes 'Gipfel/Wipfel' in
'Wanderers Nachtlied', for instance, which cannot (as sometimes
happens when sung) be reversed without obscuring the characteristically Goethean progression from the inorganic through the
organic to the human.

Quite other problems arise with the didactic ballads of Goethe's
later years, as with the equally didactic free verse of poems like
'Das Göttliche' (which I translated at the age of fifteen, but have
never revised or offered for publication in that or any version). So
direct an injunction to be 'noble and good' would meet with a wry
response from most English and American readers of poetry in
our time. The earlier Prometheus monologue is a different
matter, not only because it is a *persona* poem, but because
Promethean defiance retains its appeal in any age, and because
Goethe's genius in the vernacular triumphs in that poem over the
exemplariness of classical derivations. Altogether, the misunderstanding of Pindar's verse schemes that allowed Goethe and other
German poets to write free verse in the eighteenth century was a
happy and fruitful one, and not only for translators — as long as
the freedom led to rhapsody and colloquialism rather than to the
Winckelmannian sublime. 'Meine Göttin', with its very Goethean
mischievousness and its demotic mother-in-law, also invited
inter-cultural transfer, as the more abstract, moral and male
divinity celebrated in 'Das Göttliche' did not.

With Goethe's sonnets and elaborate stanzaic poems of later
years, often owing their peculiar solemnity to the use of feminine
end rhymes — which in English tend towards those comic effects
at which Byron excelled — there are related difficulties, aggravated
by sheer technical complexity, and by a diction at the farthest
remove from the vernacular. In translating 'Urworte. Orphisch'
— whose very title proved refractory — I had to resort to a
freedom of which Goethe availed himself elsewhere, but not in
poems of that kind. Only one of the sonnets tempted me to
grapple with those difficulties: the one on Nature and Art, so
central to the tension between freedom and order from which
much of Goethe's work sprang in all his phases. Here the multiple

rhymes of the Petrarchan sonnet did present themselves in English, but all of them, as usual, were masculine ones.

I have written elsewhere — in connection with Hölderlin — about the special resistance of English ears to adaptations of classical metres, mainly hexameters and elegiacs in Goethe's case. This antipathy could have been avoided in translating the *Roman Elegies* and a few of the *Venetian Epigrams* by transposing them into other metres or a syllabically irregular stress rhythm. But I believe that the resistance is mainly due to habit, and that it can, and should, be overcome. That the classical hexameter can be adapted quite naturally and colloquially in English for semi-narrative purposes was proved by Arthur Hugh Clough in his 'Bothie' and 'Amours de Voyage', and the same poet wrote English elegiacs and alcaics. Both of these longer poems of Clough's suggest that he must have known Goethe's *Römische Elegien,* and learnt from them. It was not the metre, but the tone and vocabulary of these elegies that proved hardest to get right consistently. With the 'Metamorphose der Pflanzen', too, the hardest thing was to strike the right balance between the vocabulary of science — in the widest sense of the word — and the vocabulary of love. For Goethe these were not at odds. For almost any other poet in German or English, especially since the Romantic period, they have belonged to wholly separate orders.

Goethe's own views on the translation of poetry seem to have undergone a characteristic metamorphosis between 1812 — when in Part III, Book 11 of *Dichtung und Wahrheit*, he advocated literal prose versions of poetic texts because the true substance ('Gehalt') of good poetry emerges most clearly when stripped of rhyme and rhythm — and 1819, when he wrote the *Noten und Abhandlungen* appended to his *West- östlicher Divan*. The earlier view is the classical one. To Dryden, too, metre and rhyme and metaphor were 'ornaments' added to the essential substance of poetry, its gist, though Dryden recognized three kinds of verse translation: metaphrase, paraphrase, and imitation. In his later passage on verse translation Goethe also posited three modes or 'epochs', distinguishing their use according to the kind of knowledge of a foreign culture each is best fitted to convey: from the literal version that allows us to assimilate it in terms of our own culture, through the 'parodistic' kind — corresponding more or less to Dryden's paraphrase, his own preferred mode — to the last and highest mode, concerned with the form and structure of the original as much as with its sense and gist. In this third 'epoch' of translation we wish to be confronted with the full peculiarity and foreignness of the translated work and attempt to 'make the translation identical with the original'. According to Goethe, this third and highest mode is also the closest possible approximation to the text itself; and the mode most appropriate to the epoch of world literature, 'Weltliteratur'. It seems right, therefore, that of Goethe's recent translators David Luke, Christopher Middleton and I have chosen Goethe's third mode, regardless of the odium of pedantry and academicism that now attaches to any attempt to render a poem's total quiddity; when from Ezra Pound to Robert Lowell it has not been Goethe's third mode but Dryden's — imitation — that has been practised by most poet-translators in our time.

For reasons already intimated, my own predilection among the many kinds of poetry written by Goethe is for those in which the form is most organic and unforced, so that the distinction between form and matter or 'content' becomes irrelevant. That is so with many of Goethe's earlier lyrics — the least translatable of his poems — but also with many of the poems of his old age. It is such poems, produced throughout Goethe's active life, that Barker Fairley had in mind when he wrote in the Introduction to his selection of Goethe's poems:

> The truth is — and this is the crowning touch — Goethe's originality is so effortless that it escapes us continually. Or rather it works its limpid spell without our being aware of what he is doing to us, till we go from him to another poet. So unartificially does he write that we forget he is writing. It is like the miracle of living, which is there all the time and we take it for granted.[3]

That quality of naturalness and seeming spontaneity — it is the 'seeming' that matters in a work of art, not the evidence of worksheets or biographical records — distinguishes Goethe the sage as much as Goethe the poet; most consistently, for me, in the many rhymed epigrams and observations, the *Sprüche*, of his later years, but also in his late and last lyrics: from those in the *West-östlicher Divan* to 'Um Mitternacht' and 'Der Bräutigam', poems that range freely across the experience and occasions of a lifetime.

Here the naturalness goes hand in hand with the wisdom, the worldly wisdom with the unworldly, the utmost seriousness with wit and even a very earthy humour. Nature and Art — where Art stands for every order that intellect, reason and will impose, Nature not only for the given world outside us but for the psychic energies that make us part of it — have here indeed been reconciled. Much of the Second Part of *Faust* belongs to that last poetic phase; but as far as Goethe's short poems are concerned, I believe it is the later work that still remains to be assimilated into the English-speaking world — and perhaps not only there. Notoriously, mint copies of the first edition of the *West-östlicher Divan* remained unsold in German bookshops as late as the First World War. Goethe was aware that no general public of his time was ready for those post-Romantic and post-Classical poems — as none was ready for Beethoven's last quartets, composed at about the same time. In the case of the *Divan*, Goethe wrote to Zelter on 17 May 1815 that both the degree of its absorption of foreign, oriental conventions and the hidden links between one poem and another made it impossible for him to send any poems that would be suitable for setting to music. We can object, of course, as Emil Staiger did, that the whole sequence is no less incomplete and enigmatic than any part of it that Goethe might have sent to Zelter; and we can point to the poem 'Gute Nacht', a kind of *envoi* to the whole sequence, that seems to contradict Goethe's doubts in the letter:

> Nun, so legt euch, liebe Lieder,
> An den Busen meinem Volke!

But to take that erotic metaphor literally as a plea for *immediate* popularity is to misunderstand the oriental conventions on which it plays, and to ignore the element of ironic playfulness so essential to much of the whole sequence. In fact it is the playfulness, rather than the recondite doctrine or private allusions, that has prevented the work as a whole from ever as yet lying very close to the German people's bosom! 'Selige Sehnsucht', which has the ease and suppleness, but lacks the ironic playfulness of other poems in the collection, has remained one of the outstanding exceptions.

Casual though many of them are, compared to the more laboured and public *Xenien,* the later rhymed epigrams could act as a bridge for English-speaking readers between Goethe the sage and Goethe the poet. Even where they make no attempt to rise above doggerel, they have the strength and flexibility of the related 'Knittelvers' in *Faust,* and cover the whole gamut of Goethe's wisdom in the fewest and plainest of words. Their precision and concision also make them eminently classical, as well as eminently memorable. It is far easier, for instance, to take in, and accept, Goethe's four lines beginning 'Wär' nicht das Auge sonnenhaft' than its prose counterparts in the scientific writings. For one thing, the epigram neither develops nor invites argument. For another, it gives pleasure — at least to readers who take pleasure in classical clarity and succinctness. Yet those four brief lines sum up one of the basic assumptions that underlie Goethe's theory of colour and all his opposition to the positivist, mechanistic science of his and our time; and they sum up his rejection of the subject-object dichotomy, a rejection as central to his artistic practice as to his theology and science. The same connections are made in the poem addressed to the physicists, 'Allerdings'; and most explicitly in 'Epirrhema', whose concluding four lines move from the 'open secret' of nature, its multiplicity and oneness, to the delight in 'serious play' that is both nature's and art's, the object's and the subject's, in Goethe's later and latest works:

> Freuet euch des wahren Scheins,
> Euch des ernsten Spieles:
> Kein Lebendiges ist ein Eins,
> Immer ists ein Vieles.

'Serious playing' is the clue to the peculiar mobility and litheness of Goethe's late poetry, including the *West-östlicher Divan* — a mobility and litheness that become explicit, too, in the more lyrical poem 'Um Mitternacht', with its progression from childhood to old age. The mobility and litheness are attributed to the third and last stage of the progression:

> Auch der Gedanke willig, sinnig, schnelle
> Sich ums Vergangne wie ums Künftige schlang;

and even the often abrupt or elliptic syntax of the late poems serves to enact the mobility of thought and reference.

In the 150 years since Goethe's death both poetry and science have grown even more specialized than they had begun to be in his own lifetime. Because that degree of specialization is scarcely compatible with wisdom of any kind, least of all with the unifying, but multiple wisdom of Goethe, his poetry as a whole has received less and less attention from non-specialists in the English-speaking world. The reception of German literature generally in this country, and the decline of interest in it after the death of Carlyle, may have something to do with it. But if Goethe's international standing had indeed been comparable to Dante's or Shakespeare's — if a considerable part of his work had been available and familiar to the generations of British intellectuals who showed their sophistication by sneering at 'Teutonic' heaviness and humourlessness —those historical shifts would not have affected Goethe. Throughout that period there were English-speaking writers and critics free from those fashionable attitudes; and German works that proved immune to them. Sheer ignorance of Goethe's work beyond *Faust,* the conversations with Eckermann, *Werther* and perhaps *Wilhelm Meisters Lehrjahre* during part of that period, is the main cause. That ignorance in turn has to do with the specialization, the predominance of the Romantic-Symbolist aesthetic in the arts, and a parallel trend towards fragmented autonomy in the sciences.

Although one would have to be very reckless indeed to make any prediction whatever about developments in the arts or sciences, when their very continuance is threatened by the specialization that Goethe opposed, Romantic-Symbolist assumptions have certainly lost or loosened their hold on the arts, and more and more scientists have grown aware of the dangers of disciplines and techniques pursued in isolation — and in blind indifference to the effects of their application. Nineteenth-century notions of greatness and grandeur that may have helped to turn Goethe into a national and educational institution in Germany — involving also, of course, a process of selection and suppression — have become equally dubious (so that it is no longer outrageous to prefer a tiny sonata by Scarlatti to a 'grand sonata' by one of the later Romantics). If Goethe's wisdom and Goethe's art had been as educationally effective as they were made out to be, his own work would have served to invalidate some of those criteria of grandeur:

> Und es ist das ewig Eine,
> Das sich vielfach offenbart:
> Klein das Grosse, gross das Kleine,
> Alles nach der eignen Art;

— to quote another of those late little poems which ought to be, but are not, as proverbial as Goethe would have liked them to become. Those small poems and epigrams cock all sorts of snooks at the attitudes which allowed Goethe to be presented as an 'Olympian' and a national monument. For they are as personal as they are impersonal (or trans-personal); as subjective as they are objective; as occasional as they are central to Goethe's constant and deepest concerns.

For all the political conservatism that has been imputed to the later Goethe — another dubious simplification, like Thomas Mann's projection on to Goethe of his own sense of being a representative of the 'bourgeois age' — Goethe's faith in the constancy and mutability of nature made him, once he had resolved the antinomy of Nature and Art, a meliorist, if not an optimist, in his thinking about society too. On the one hand he affirmed tradition, to the extent of questioning the novelty of his own achievements and the uniqueness of his own person:

> . . . Sind nun die Elemente nicht
> Aus dem Komplex zu trennen,
> Was ist denn an dem ganzen Wicht
> Original zu nennen?

On the other hand, he could write his lines on the United States of America — 'Amerika, du hast es besser' —approving the American Revolution and advising American writers to make the best of their clean slate by avoiding the Romantic cult of knight, highwayman and ghost stories. America, of course, was to develop its own heroic lore and its own conservatism — a development that would not have astonished Goethe, consistent as it is with his large and impartial view of human affairs.

Though it may be difficult today to adopt such a view, now that nature and civilization are more critically in conflict than Goethe had any grounds for thinking it possible for them to be (even if he was almost alone in his time in recognizing the roots of that possibility), Goethe's later work has acquired a new significance and relevance. By stripping much of his later poetry of metaphor

and merely emotive effects — of that quality of vagueness which
Baudelaire saw as indispensable to the beauty of Romantic art —
Goethe defied the taste of his age. Even his descents into a low
vernacular have their parallel in our own century in the practice of
Brecht, whose later poetry has the same hardness, spareness and
seeming ordinariness, in conscious defiance of the Romantic-
Symbolist aesthetic —and with a related awareness that the first
person singular need not be avoided in poetry as long as its
singularity is not overrated:

> Dich prüfe nur allermeist,
> Ob du Kern oder Schale seist.

Both the later Brecht and the later Goethe have come up against a
wide-spread, and most understandable, distrust of didacticism in
poetry; both could disarm it by their take-it-or-leave-it casualness
and the avoidance of emotive rhetoric. Both were masters of the
truly classical art that consists in concealing art.

Goethe's unifying concept of entelechy, metamorphosis and
growth, like the related one of subject-object reciprocity, has
seeped into general awareness less from his poetry than from his
scientific tracts and the *Maximen und Reflexionen,* prose aphorisms
more or less concurrent with the late verse. In many cases it is not
through his own works at all, but through the medium of
psychology, or movements such as Rudolf Steiner's anthroposophy,
that Goethe's unifying principle has impinged on our consciousness. Much of his literary influence, even on English poets like
Arthur Hugh Clough and Matthew Arnold, may well have been as
indirect and elusive as the influence of his wisdom. That is in the
nature of influences; and I have already suggested that there was
something in Goethe's entire work that aspired to the condition of
anonymity — even if there is scarcely another writer whose
person has been as minutely recorded and studied.

In putting a special emphasis here on Goethe's later verse —
including that part of it which makes the least claim to being great
or monumental, or that part of it, the *West-östlicher Divan,* in which
the former author of *Werther* was at the farthest remove from
collaboration with the *Zeitgeist,* though not from collaboration
with Nature or his other goddess, Imagination — the last thing I
intended was yet again to play off Goethe the sage against Goethe
the poet. On the contrary: what I wish to suggest is that in the later

work the two are indivisibly fused; and fused in a way that has to do with the aesthetic (and aesthetics) as much as with knowledge and wisdom in other domains. Nor would Goethe have bothered to write those little epigrammatic observations in rhyme if they had been mere duplications of what can be said, and had been said, in the prose of his tracts or prose aphorisms. If we read them as poetry — and I believe we should — their form and diction must be as essential to what they are and do as the form and diction of 'Über allen Gipfeln' is to that brief poem. Indeed a common factor of compression and reduction contributes to the pleasure to be derived from either kind of poem. Because Goethe was less a 'nature poet' than a poet of nature — human as much as non-human — another common feature is the classical generality of the images in both kinds of poem. Where Goethe had no compelling reason to 'number the streaks of the tulip', as he had in 'Die Metamorphose der Pflanzen', he could make do in lyrical poems with 'Gipfel', 'Wipfel', 'Vögelein' — unspecified, un-described. Whereas even Hölderlin, not to mention Wordsworth, had begun to worry over the names of trees in his later poems. According to Samuel Johnson, 'the business of a poet is to examine, not the individual, but the species, to remark general properties and large appearances . . . He is to exhibit in his portraits of nature such prominent and striking features, as recall the original to every mind; and must neglect the minuter discriminations'. That is the classical prescription. Needless to say, Goethe felt under no obligation to observe it consistently, in his so-called 'classical' phase or in any other. In parts of the *West-östlicher Divan* the opposite principle of minuteness is at work — or at play. In the sensuous poem 'Versunken', for instance, with its proto-Baudelairean exploration of a 'hemisphere in a head of hair'.

The succinctness and colloquialism of the rhymed epigrams is no easier to render in English than the more elaborate and ingenious artistry of some of the poems in the *Divan*. But some liberties can be taken with both the literal sense and the rhyme schemes in those cases where the originals, too, have something of the character of improvisation. The range of tone and theme in the epigrams — from the arcanely wise to the demotically wisecracking — is such that no translator is likely to be able, or even willing, to render them all; and those bearing on ethics or on

Christian dogma remain as controversial as when they were written. This strikes me as another good reason for including a generous selection from them, as well as from the late lyrics, in any new English edition that could make Goethe more than a respected, but largely unread, world classic. Wordsworth and Coleridge did Goethe the honour of quarrelling with what to them was a pagan immoralism or amoralism in his work — out of a prejudice that T.S. Eliot also voiced in his early dismissal of Goethe, though without the excuse of taking him seriously.

A new English edition of Goethe's selected works is at last being prepared. My hope is that its editors will not make the mistake of selecting only the least controversial works. Those in which Goethe's humanism is most idealized and stylized, as in some of those poems which the Hamburg edition calls 'die grossen Hymnen'; or those plays in which Goethe's classicizing is farthest from the vernacular, the true source of his classicism at all periods of his working life. Goethe's own judgment of his *Iphigenie*, one of his most painstakingly exemplary works, as 'verteufelt human' should be heeded at last, now that no monument is safe on its pedestal and the plaster-cast models have been put away. The German word for 'humanity', it should also be remembered, is not 'Humanität' but 'Menschlichkeit'. A merely human Goethe, whose humanity embraced every kind of contradiction, ranging far and wide, high and low, affirming, celebrating all that he saw and imagined, but was not above making fun of anything contrary to human or non-human nature: such a Goethe could have a better chance in the museum of world literature, more and more overcrowded with exhibits, as it is, while the attendance falls.

It is this humanity that Goethe presents in his two small *Grabschriften* — so small that no room was found for them in the Hamburg edition. If the note in the Jubiläumsausgabe (II, 324) is not out of date, the first of these epitaphs was written in Goethe's twenties, the second late in life. If so, his imagination proved as reliable as his experience. In any case, the two both contradict and complement each other.

1

Ich war ein Knabe warm und gut,
Als Jüngling hatt' ich frisches Blut,
Versprach einst einen Mann.

Gelitten hab' ich und geliebt
Und liege nieder ohnbetrübt,
Da ich nicht weiter kann.

2

Als Knabe verschlossen und trutzig,
Als Jüngling anmasslich und stutzig,
Als Mann zu Taten willig,
Als Greis leichtsinnig und grillig! —
Auf deinem Grabstein wird man lesen:
Das ist fürwahr ein Mensch gewesen.

Notes to A Perilous Multiplicity

1.   In *Meisterwerke deutscher Sprache* (Zurich, 1948²), pp. 119-35.

2.   *GLL*, 2 (1949); reprinted in *Goethe. Poet and Thinker*, pp. 20-34.

3.   *Goethe, Selected Poems,* edited by Barker Fairley (London, Heinemann, 1954), p. xv.

On not being Intimidated: Socialist Overhauling of a Classic   Philip Brady

On 12 April 1921 the young Bertolt Brecht, out on the spree in Augsburg with his brother Walter, called on an acquaintance, who makes this one brief appearance in Brecht's diary:

> Ich gehe . . . mit Walter zu einem kleinen philiströsen Weinschläuchlein, dem Ingenieur Helm, der von Goethe schwärmt und Ideale an Schnüren wie Drachen fliegen lässt.

Such is Brecht's first recorded encounter with a lover of Goethe. No second visit to the philistine, wine-swilling flier of ideals is recorded — perhaps Brecht needed no further reminder of the seductive power of Goethe over idealists. It may, however, have been an unknown successor to engineer Helm who, some five years later, provoked a crisp little note, still unpublished, 'Goethe kein ausreichender ersatz für den lieben gott'. Soon after this Brecht, no doubt with engineer Helm and his successors in mind, took to referring irreverently to Goethe, in a strongly Bavarian accent, as 'Goethinger'.

Brecht is objecting not to Goethe but to Goethe-cults, to that genuflecting 'Muckertum im Goethekultus' that Gottfried Keller had identified as truly philistine in 1884. Hence by the mid-1920's he is proposing, as an alternative to hero-worship, something bereft of respect and fine feelings: 'Schnoddrigkeit'. Only thus — and the locution is calculatedly down-to-earth — can the 'Materialwert' of a work like Goethe's *Faust* be extracted. But earlier than this Brecht had put Goethe to practical use. The

'Sieben Hasen' was a brothel in Augsburg. There, early in 1919, Brecht heard a prostitute standing on a table singing obscene songs. He capped her performance, reducing her and everyone else to stunned silence, by singing 'Der Gott und die Bajadere'. A stranger was moved to collect money for Brecht, and Brecht himself was persuaded to sing the whole ballad once again. On other jaunts he liked to sing 'Der Rattenfänger', and it is not difficult to imagine the symbiosis between Goethe's pied piper and Brecht reaching a climax in the third and final verse of Goethe's poem, which so perfectly matches, in manner and in substance, Brecht's view of himself:

> Dann ist der vielgewandte Sänger
> Gelegentlich ein Mädchenfänger;
> In keinem Städtchen langt' er an,
> Wo er's nicht mancher angethan.
> Und wären Mädchen noch so blöde,
> Und wären Weiber noch so spröde,
> Doch allen wird so liebebang
> Bei Zaubersaiten und Gesang.

Goethe, often an unfamiliar Goethe, came to serve Brecht in a variety of situations. There was no room for 'Mahomets Gesang' (Brecht's comment, this time in Berlin German, is destructively obvious, 'det Janze stelltn Strom dar, hastenichjemerktwa?'); but there was room, and this on the day after his *Arbeitsjournal* records Hitler's assault on Warsaw, for the following:

> Ich blättere in goethes PANDORA und bin wieder betroffen über die HIRTENGESÄNGE, wie sich da das verfeinerte mit dem primitiven berührt!

Later, when those troubles were over, it is again the unusual choice in the unusual context which impresses. On 18 December 1948 Brecht, newly arrived in East Berlin, describes his daily routine: up at half past five, coffee or tea, then Georg Lukács or Goethe, and, if Goethe, then *Der Sammler und die Seinigen,* Goethe's lively plea for a marriage of 'Ernst' and 'Spiel' in the visual arts. Perhaps Brecht was re-stocking his own repertoire of bêtes-noires from Goethe's catalogue of myopic approaches to the arts: the 'Kopisten', the 'Poetisierer', the 'Nebulisten', the 'Schwebler und Nebler'.

These are scattered examples of an unorthodox encounter with Goethe; and they are important because they are the fruits of a refusal to idealize, a refusal to stay within the canon of familiar, classic texts. Moreover the encounter —which, for my purpose, begins on the spree in Augsburg —does not end with *Der Sammler* at five-thirty in the morning in late 1948. There is a further crucial and singularly explicit phase from which I derive part of my title. In 1954 Brecht published what might be said to be — he died two years later — a concluding gloss on that lifelong relationship with 'Goethinger'. It is the essay 'Einschüchterung durch die Klassizität'. Brecht is disturbed by the baleful influence of those who are reduced to a kind of unproductive awe by the sight of a classic writer. Such awe, besides imposing a spurious, barren greatness from outside, effectively drains the literary classic of its 'ursprüngliche Frische'. The essay is clearer perhaps about general goals than about precise methods, but it gains precision from its context. The time was 1953/4, the place East Berlin; and in this place at that time questions touched on by Brecht were under urgent, widespread, official debate. Time and place were giving Brecht's piece an added, topical sharpness of focus.

It is not necessary to unravel the complexities of the debate to which Brecht was contributing. The debate has been chronicled, and some of its key-terms — 'Humanismus', 'Tradition', 'Aneignung des klassischen Erbes' — have become permanent features in the East German cultural landscape.[1] In 1953, when Brecht was writing his essay, they were still in process of promulgation, a process set markedly in train by the 1949 celebrations of the Goethe-year. An official declaration of that year, typical of many, was unambiguous in its claim:

> Die SED steht an der Spitze aller fortschrittlichen Kräfte im Kampf um eine neue Kultur, die an das grosse kulturelle Erbe des klassischen deutschen Humanismus anknüpft und dabei besonders den tiefen demokratischen und humanistischen Gehalt lebendig gestaltet, der aus Goethes Werk zu uns spricht.

Brecht might well have felt the presence again, this time *en masse* and organized, of engineer Helm flying his ideals like kites. The rhetorical forms, the mingling of slogan and prescription, the thinking in superlatives — above all perhaps the absence of

radical questioning — make of Goethe a figure of intimidating
stature, make him (to adopt a distinction of Brecht's) not
'volkstümlich' but 'funktionärstümlich', encouraging reverence
rather than that 'Fähigkeit des kritischen Geniessens' which
Brecht saw as essential in any approach to the classics.

In 1953 there was, however, a further element, giving a
personal accent to Brecht's arguments against being intimidated
by the likes of Goethe. His essay and the notes which accompany
it are the by-product of his sole attempt to produce a Goethe play,
namely the *Urfaust*. The result of this uniquely public confrontation
between Brecht and Goethe was, according to Manfred Wekwerth,
who was present at rehearsals and discussions, 'eine der inter-
essantesten und theatergeschichtlich wichtigsten Arbeiten von
Brecht'.[2] Moreover, it was a controversial production, withdrawn
after nineteen performances, and the sound of controversy
reached Walter Ulbricht, who found it intolerable 'dass man die
grossen Ideen in Goethes *Faust* zu einer Karikatur macht'.[3]

There are two stages to Brecht's involvement with the *Urfaust*
and they illustrate two different escape-routes from 'Einschüchterung'. The first stage led to a studio-production in Potsdam in
April 1952. Anxious, on his own admission, to counteract
traditional presentations of Faust, Brecht produced what Manfred
Wekwerth saw as a polemical reading, underlining Faust's
depravity and his criminal adventurousness. The order of scenes
was changed in order to accelerate Faust's attachment to Gretchen;
as an entry in Brecht's *Arbeitsjournal* for 6 April 1952 notes, 'die
parasitäre, auf rücksichtslosen genuss gehende liebe faustens
wird schärfer gekennzeichnet'. For Goethe's step-by-step account
Brecht had, it seems, substituted shock-effects.

Brecht's misgivings were prompt, his second thoughts drastic.
The order of scenes was restored, polemic was abandoned for
ambiguity, for the 'Dialektik', the 'Humor', the 'Lust am Neuen'
which Brecht had discerned in Goethe's text. Brecht summarized
this second attempt:

> Erst jetzt, in einer völligen Neuinszenierung, wurde
> versucht, der so grossartigen Widersprüchlichkeit der
> Goetheschen Faustfigur gerecht zu werden und ihr das
> Positive zu verleihen, die Humanität, Radikalität in
> Denken und Fühlen, die innere Weite, durch die sie tief
> in das Bewusstsein der Deutschen eingedrungen ist.

We can reconstruct something of that second production from Brecht's notes and Wekwerth's detailed commentary. Faust had regained his stature, now he was a 'grosser Fachmann', summoning up the Erdgeist in a grand conjuration accompanied by music (in the first production he had been furtive). The contradictions were made visual — the desire for life vitiated by visible clumsiness ('linkisch' is Wekwerth's recurrent term) when faced with life — 'der Professor kommt durch'; throughout the play Faust moved with the 'steife, aufrechte Haltung des grossen Gelehrten' but spoke in a 'matter Ton'. Particular moments aimed to open up, rather than obscure, general meanings — Mephisto's treatment of the Schüler was now humourless (the first production sought crude humour), and the scene was to show not the weakness of a particular scholar but a general consequence: 'Solche Lehrer richten die Jugend zugrunde'. Faust answering Gretchen's questions about his religion was the intellectual using knowledge as a means of seduction.

These are shifts of emphasis, achieved through the painstaking discussions, recorded by Wekwerth, which amount to Brecht's most elaborate examination of any work of Goethe's. This second production, however, took bolder steps outside the realm of production. The play now opened with a 'Vorspruch', in which Mephisto, emphatically an 'Unterteufel' and sporting flashy golden horns, introduced himself and Faust to music by Paul Dessau and in words drawn from Goethe's 1818 *Maskenzug*. It is, so to speak, a stroke of cooperative genius that makes Goethe supply the words for a Brechtian production. Mephisto presents Faust to the audience:

> Hier steht ein Mann, ihr seht's ihm an,
> In Wissenschaften hat er gnug getan,
> Wie dieses Vieleck, das er trägt,
> Beweist er habe sich auf vielerlei gelegt.
> Doch da er Kenntnis gnug erworben,
> Ist er der Welt fast abgestorben.
> Auch ist, um resolut zu handeln,
> Mit heiterm Angesicht zu wandeln,
> Sein Äussres nicht von rechter Art,
> Zu lang der Rock, zu kraus der Bart . . . (WA, i, XVI, 286)

An addition later in the play goes outside Goethe, but not very far. The *Urfaust* lacks the pact with the Devil, and Brecht wished to fill the gap. For this he needed not the poetry of *Faust Erster Teil* but a text which would supply narrative details without any sublime enhancing of the issues. He chose to have read out, but not acted out, lines from the *Puppenspiel,* thus making stylistically explicit the contrasts which he had already detected and praised in Goethe's own text:

> Diese Fabel, welch ein Wurf! Der Einfall allein, den hochaktuellen Stoff von der Kindesmörderin mit dem alten *Puppenspiel vom Dr. Faustus* zu verknüpfen! Diese Sprache: der Hans-Sachs-Vers grobianischer Prägung, gepaart mit der neuen, humanistischen Prosa!

The textual additions confirm what production details, along with Wekwerth's record of discussions, already have suggested — Brecht had, as Werner Mittenzwei has put it, rediscovered the 'Dialektiker' in Goethe.

   It was entirely typical of Brecht, although it surprised everyone at the time, that he decided to provoke argument about the element of materialism in Goethe by asking assistants working on the production of the *Urfaust* to read the *West-östlicher Divan*. If he asked questions of Goethe —and Brecht was, in Wekwerth's view, 'Ermunterung zum Denken in Person' — it was in the expectation that Goethe would supply the answers. And the questions, I have suggested, were born of a lifelong refusal to be intimidated, a refusal to leave unexamined the area of overlap between Goethe and the here-and-now. Clearly Goethe had survived Brecht's questions very well, standing him in good stead from the time when a stanza from 'Der Rattenfänger' could give classic sanction to sexual escapades to the time when the *Urfaust* took him to the centre of a public debate about the status of Goethe in a socialist society. That debate has never ceased, even though the rhetoric has been pared down and the prescriptive tone has grown more subtle. It is impossible to say how far others have been influenced by what the East German scholar Hans Kaufmann has called 'Brechts — gelinde gesagt — gespanntes Verhältnis zu Goethe'. But certainly other socialist writers, in their different ways, and differently acknowledging Brecht's initiatives, have refused to be intimidated either by the debate itself or by Goethe. Two such writers, each distinctive, each different from Brecht, Volker Braun and Peter Hacks, illustrate some of the alternatives.

An East German critic, Silvia Schlenstedt, interviewing Volker Braun in 1972, described his use of Goethe as

> das Hereinnehmen von einzelnen Bildern und Wendungen, die verschoben, umgekehrt, variiert werden, so dass Alte als Unterlage noch durchscheint, aber durch die sprachliche Arbeit das Umarbeiten, Umkehren, Verwerfen früherer Haltungen und Lagen erkennbar wird.

Braun's own preferred term, in the same interview, is 'Umkehrung', denoting not simply a radical approach to the literary classic but radical social changes — 'sie drückt den gesellschaftlichen Vorgang aus, dass die Verhältnisse vom Kopf auf die Füsse gestellt werden'. This, in other words, is not Goethe adapted but Goethe recollected from a distance, 'als Zitat, als heitere Erinnerung', as Braun puts it. Braun is commenting on Goethe's presence in *Hinze und Kunze*, a play which in its first version, performed in 1968, was more pointedly titled *Hans Faust*.

The contours of Goethe's *Faust* are still discernible in Braun's play in the relationship between Hinze, a restless building worker, whose energies are frustrated, and Kunze, a 'Bauleiter', offering a new beginning. The issues are real enough; but Braun's language, an irregular blank verse during most of the play, is pitched above the everyday — halfway, so to speak, towards Goethe's grander gestures. Thus Hinze accepts Kunze's offer of help and vows:

> Solang wir nicht zufrieden sind, bleiben wir
> Zusammen, und der vorher aufhört
> Und den andern im Stich lässt — der soll draufgehn
> Im grauen Alltag und vergessen sein —

Again, when Hinze declares his goals, he does so in a speech which echoes Schiller, quotes Goethe — and overturns both:

> Der Starke ist am schwächsten allein. Dünkel
> Alles selbst zu wissen! zu faul hinzuhören.
> Eingeklemmt zwischen Helm und Plattfuss
> Der gute Mensch in seinem dunklen Drang —
> Das ist alles verflucht, ich lass alles sein.

Braun is not, however, simply playing with an audience's half-recollected stock of *Faust* quotations, he is relying on more general recollections of plot and character. Thus a concealed quotation in the first scene is a clue to these more far-reaching connections — Kunze, the Mephisto-figure, surveys a desolate site and urges Hinze to action:

> Auf dem freien Grund
> Bedeckt von Trümmern, wimmelt
> Das freie Volk, in seinem Dreck gefangen.

We are close to the end of *Faust Zweiter Teil* and to the lines in Faust's final speech:

> Solch ein Gewimmel möcht' ich sehn,
> Auf freiem Grund mit freiem Volke stehn.
>
> (lines 11579-80)

Braun is beginning where Goethe ends, following into practice what the hundred-year-old Faust proclaims as a goal: 'Arbeiter schaffe Meng' auf Menge' (line 11522).

There are other 'Umkehrungen' of plot and character. It is a neat reversal of Goethe's plot that has Faust later advised by Mephisto to study, in order to equip himself for effective action. When he complains after six months at his books he echoes Goethe's Faust, but the echoes are faint and they serve to point up a contrast:

> Der Rücken
> Brennt, die Hände schwimmen auf
> Endlosem Papier, Buchstaben
> Ans Auge genagelt. Ich seh nicht mehr, ich
> Begreif nichts.
> *Schweigen.*
> Kann mir da einer helfen?

There is, too, a Gretchen-figure, Marlies; she too is pregnant, she too destroys the child — by abortion. She it is, however, who is the creative force, beginning to build the new society which Hinze, with his wild egocentricity, jeopardizes. When Hinze returns to Marlies at the end, with every prospect of success under her guidance — 'Ich muss von vorn beginnen' — Braun has recaptured the implication of Gretchen's closing words 'Vergönne mir, ihn zu belehren' (line 12092).

Braun, it might be said, overhauls Goethe in one sense, in that he leaves him behind; but he hardly overhauls him in the other — Brecht's — sense of refurbishing and renovating. And yet *Hinze und Kunze* needs its substructural relationship with Goethe's *Faust* if its irony and its modernity are to emerge with any clarity.

At this same time, in the late 1960's, Braun, working on a smaller scale, had kept Goethe perhaps more recognizably present in his revision of 'Prometheus'. To revise Goethe's 'Prometheus' is tantamount to revising socialist iconography, since Goethe's poem, endlessly reprinted, illustrated and imitated, had long been the archetypal image of defiant, Revolutionary Man. It was indeed as 'Goethe-Prometheus' that the Socialist press had chosen to celebrate Goethe in 1899, the one hundred and fiftieth anniversary of his birth.[4] Braun retains Goethe's form — a seven-stanza ode — but transforms the legend. The new Prometheus has become the astronaut, carrying fire not down but up to heaven. An individual still speaks — 'Ich fliege am Himmel' — but his strength, his defiant rejection of apathy, derives from a socialist world of 'wir' and 'unser' —'Was glaub ich denn/ Wenn nicht an uns?'

Goethe survives most obviously in Braun's poem in the form and in the momentum of defiant assertion and rhetorical question. But Braun may be paying Goethe a further, oblique compliment. Like Goethe he had planned a Prometheus-drama but he made no progress. Goethe, on the other hand, produced a fragment which, in the 1830 edition, concludes with the ode. In that fragment, however, there is a call to active construction worlds away from the lofty tones of the ode. Here, if anywhere, Braun's Prometheus has his counterpart, when Goethe's hero instructs a man who has entered bearing trees how to build a dwelling. For the eighteenth century that first hut, Rousseau's 'première révolution', was richly symbolic, but Prometheus's instruction is practical and strikingly plain:

> Erst ab die Äste! —
> Dann hier rammle diesen
> Schief in den Boden hier
> Und diesen hier, so gegenüber;
> Und oben verbinde sie! —
> Dann wieder zwei hier hinten hin
> Und oben einen quer darüber.

> Nun die Äste herab von oben
> Bis zur Erde,
> Verbunden und verschlungen die,
> Und Rasen ringsumher . . . .   (HA, IV, 183)

Braun's oblique strategy in both his play and his Prometheus-
poem may seem ruthlessly selective, but it could nevertheless be
said to presuppose Goethe's relevance. It is the mixture of
distance and affinity which seems to attract him, and this he has
given semi-autobiographical, semi-fictional treatment in a prose
work, *Der Hörsaal,* first published in 1964 and republished in 1972
as the second part of *Das ungezwungne Leben Kasts.* Hans Kast,
whose circumstances overlap markedly with Braun's own, is a
student of philosophy. At the start he is buried in books and
uneasy: 'die Bücher stapelten sich auf dem Fussboden, die Sätze
und Seiten füllten den Kopf aus — ich kam zu nichts sonst!
Irgend etwas fehlte . . .'. He reads Lamettrie's *Der Mensch eine
Maschine* in the seminar-library, seated in such a way that he can
see the back of the neck of a beautiful girl whilst reading such lines
as 'So geliebt & begehrt die Sinnenlust auch sein mag . . . so
verschafft sie uns doch nur einen einmaligen Genuss, der
zugleich ihr Grab ist'. When he sees her face he loses his
composure. Books in general, eighteenth-century mechanistics in
particular, offer little defence against a pretty face. What seem
merest hints of a Faustian situation gain substance next day when
Kast meets the girl in a lecture on the *Urfaust* by a certain Professor
R. His first encounter takes place to the accompaniment of a trite
account of Goethe's play:

> R. herein, Getrommel auf den Bänken. Ich winkte dem
> Mädchen, es nickte wie selbstverständlich, zwängte sich
> durch die Reihe. Es setzte sich neben mich. Also Urfaust.
> Der schnelle Redefluss R.'s, in jedem Satz riss er Wissen
> zusammen aus drei Büchern, und aus dem Vollen
> schöpfkellenweise über die Köpfe gegossen. Eine seltsame
> Arbeit: das nur in sich hineinsacken lassen und langsam
> wieder aufbaun in den Hirnzellen, der Kopf dröhnt,
> oder schmerzt. Faust, ursprünglich als Universitätssatire,
> Gottsched-Parodie. Szenerie führt dahin. Auerbachs
> Keller. Das Mädchen pinselte mit, ich sah nur ihre
> Hand. Unmöglichkeit eines Selbsthelfers in anarchischer

Zeit. Gretchentragödie. Sie ist schön, sah ich, ihre Lippen voll und rot, die Stirn schön gewölbt, die Augen, die Lippen . . . . Ungleichheit der Liebenden, wegen Ungleichheit der Stände. ·

Kast's interest grows as Professor R. plods through Goethe. By the time the lecture finishes Kast has made a date. Life has triumphed over the academic. But Goethe, who seems to inhabit, with Lamettrie, the same bookish world that stifles Kast, is in fact closer to Kast's emotional life. Linde, the girl, tender, devoted, planning for domesticity, Kast restless, incapable of single-minded devotion ('ich fühlte zu viele Menschen in der Brust') — the parallels to Gretchen and Faust are obvious. Professor R.'s doggedly common-place account of the *Urfaust* divorced Goethe from the life of Kast, but only temporarily, because Kast's own later life rebuilds the connection with Goethe. Life, in other words, rather than an academic's exegesis, demonstrates the relevance of the *Urfaust.*

It is impossible not to be reminded of that later, more famous encounter between a younger generation and Goethe in the shape of Ulrich Plenzdorf's *Die Neuen Leiden des jungen W.* There the encounter is less auspicious —Plenzdorf's Edgar Wibeau en-counters *Werther* not in a lecture-hall but as a tatty paperback in the dark in a ramshackle outside-lavatory. The convergence of two disparate lives — Werther's and Edgar Wibeau's — is a more complex affair than Kast's living-out of the *Urfaust.* In both cases, however, Goethe has been reasserted against the odds. Plenzdorf's novel is not my subject, but it is important because in a recent story, *Unvollendete Geschichte* (1975), Braun has briefly brought Goethe, Plenzdorf and the protracted, much documented debate about Plenzdorf[5] into the crisis of his central character, Karin, the eighteen-year-old daughter of a local dignitary. Told by her parents to break off for no clear reason all contact with her boyfriend Frank, she has surrendered. Between the surrender and the discovery that Frank has attempted suicide she lights on a book belonging to her brother. The episode is worth quoting:

Sie hatte von dem Buch gehört, allein das Wort *Leiden* im Titel war erschreckend genug. In der Zeitung hatte gestanden, der Verfasser versuche, seine eigenen Leiden der Gesellschaft 'aufzuoktroyieren'. Das wäre, dachte sie jetzt, immerhin neu, dass das Leid des einzelnen die Gesellschaft stören würde.

Karin likes the story, noting that her brother had written 'Ja!' and
'Genau!' frequently in the margin. But she feels that Edgar's fate
does not connect with her own — 'sie verstand ihn, aber verstand
sich davon nicht besser'. Thinking about Edgar brings her back to
the *Werther* she had studied at school:

> der Werther, den er immer zitierte, hing noch anders mit
> der Welt zusammen. Das hatten sie in der Schule
> behandelt. Der stiess sich an ihrem Kern. W. stiess sich
> an allem Äusseren, das war lustig, und ging per Zufall
> über den Jordan. Das Ungeheure in dem *Werther* war,
> dass da ein Riss durch die Welt ging und durch ihn selbst.
> Das war eine alte Zeit.

Braun's fictional eighteen-year-old with a Werther-like crisis on
her hands has entered the current non-fictional debate and has
found a paradigmatic completeness in *Werther* lacking in his
topical counterpart. Only its East German setting, where private
responses to Goethe can become public issues, can give such an
episode its ironic flavour. For there is irony in the fact that a
teenage girl, unintimidated by the 'alte Zeit' and seemingly
unaware of obstacles to 'Aneignung', can enter so straightforward
a plea for *Werther*.

In the same year that Volker Braun's Karin spoke up for *Werther*
the case for letting Goethe speak for himself was argued in a
different quarter. The argument was to prove less simple, because
it was a prelude to a different kind of overhauling, directed to a
different kind of Goethe. Peter Hacks, the writer in question,
believing that havoc was wrought by the unintimidated in their
tamperings with classic texts, begins his essay 'Über das Revidieren
von Klassikern' with a joke. A hare racing through the countryside
is joined by a second hare. They run in silence for a few hundred
miles, whereupon the second hare asks, 'What are we running
away from?' 'They have passed a law that all hares will have their
fifth leg sawn off.' 'But we've only got four.' 'You don't know
them — first they saw, then they count.' 'Ich habe nichts vor', thus
runs Hacks's gloss, 'als mich zum Nachteil derjenigen Sorte von
Bearbeitungen zu äussern, welche sägt, bevor sie gezählt hat.'
There is already more than a hint of polemic in this, and indeed
Hacks provokingly simplifies the issues. The literary classic, he
argues, is a classic precisely because it makes sense. Nor does he

deny that, in protecting the classics against marauding adapters, he is in effect conferring on them a degree of impregnable sovereignty. In his closing words Hacks argues for incense and pedestals:

> Ich will die Klassiker ungetadelt, nicht unangewendet. Ich will sie beweihräuchert und verstanden. Ich glaube an sie; denn ich habe die Erfahrung gemacht, dass sie mich niemals im Stich lassen.

> Und man sollte sie nicht auf einen Sockel stellen? Gewiss nicht. Sie stehen da längst. Wer das nicht sehen kann, weiss seinen Platz nicht.

This is not the language of East Germany's official custodians of the cultural heritage; indeed Hacks's plea for reverence has little in common with the forms of reverence and understanding advocated by the makers of cultural policy. It could be said that Hacks, far from contributing to the public discussion, is in effect turning his back on it. But the essay is itself at one point less rigorous than its assertive conclusion suggests: there is an area where the classic text needs revision, needs an injection of life — 'Bearbeitet werden darf nur ein Stück, das in irgendeiner Hinsicht Fragment ist'. The task is not an easy one; it presupposes indeed, in Hacks's view, a rare measure of collaborative kinship; but the collaboration is less likely to destroy, more likely to enhance.

If in theory Peter Hacks appears to be restoring old-fashioned, larger-than-life grandeur to the classic writer, in practice he scrupulously avoids those well-known works by Goethe which have provided the grandeur in the first place. Three plays have Goethe variously as their subject; two adapt works which have never fallen within any canon, socialist or non-socialist; the third has as its subject, not any work, but Goethe himself. The adaptations are *Das Jahrmarktsfest zu Plundersweilern,* a work first published in the same year as the essay 'Über das Revidieren von Klassikern', and *Pandora, Drama nach J.W. von Goethe,* published in 1981. The third play, which Hacks has described, not altogether helpfully, as 'ein Zweipersonenstück, welches in Wirklichkeit ein Einpersonenstück ist, das in Wirklichkeit ein Zweipersonenstück ist', is *Ein Gespräch im Hause Stein über den abwesenden Herrn von Goethe,* first published in 1977.

It might be said that the *Jahrmarktsfest,* a 'Schönbartspiel' of

1774/78 (WA, i, XVI, 7ff.) and *Pandora,* a 'Festspiel' of 1807/08 (HA, V, 332 ff.), have little in common beyond the fact that both were left incomplete by Goethe. Each has its own texture of contrasts and polarities: in *Pandora* 'Systole und Diastole des Weltgeistes', as Riemer noted in his diary (HA, V, 521); in the *Jahrmarktsfest* comic contrasts generated not least by the play-within-a-play structure, the mock-heroic Esther-play acted at a fair. Nor does Hacks minimize the differences: 'Festspiel' and 'Schönbartspiel' remain far apart, each completed and yet left intact.

Goethe's own *Jahrmarktsfest zu Plundersweilern,* to begin with the earlier of the two adaptations, has, besides the concealed ironies and parodies discoverable by Goethe's immediate circle, humorous effects of a more accessible kind. Goethe has made of the Esther-Haman-Mardochai story, in which Haman the anti-semite seeks the death of Mardochai and all his race, a burlesque in heroic verse. He has, at the same time, for all the playful context of the fairground and the histrionics of the acting-troupe, preserved a hint of frisson at anti-semitism rampant. But the promised tragedy, the 'Tragödia /Voll süsser Worten und Sittensprüchen' (lines 20-21), is kept at arm's length. King Ahasver, warned of danger, threatens genocide:

> Nun soll's der ganzen Welt vor meinem Zorne Grauen!
> Geh, lass mir auf einmal zehntausend Galgen bauen.
>
> (lines 374-5)

But Haman, for all his villainy — and it is he who has fomented the weakling king's anger — has a sense of economic priorities and urges moderation:

> Unüberwindlichster! Hier lieg' ich, bitte Gnad'!
> Es wär' um's viele Volk — und um die Waldung Schad'
>
> (lines 376-7)

When Mardochai pleads with Esther to intercede on his behalf with the king his vision of his own dead body is comic:

> Dort nascht geschäftig mir, zum Winter-Zeitvertreib,
> Ein garstig Rabenvolk das schöne Fett vom Leib!
>
> (lines 517-8)

Whilst Esther solicitously offers very cold comfort:

Doch kann ich es erlangen,
So sollst du mir nicht lang am leid'gen Galgen hangen.
(lines 523-4)

It is worth emphasizing the comic incongruities in Goethe's original because Hacks is clearly at pains to develop them. He has retained the black comedy, the pathos, the mock-heroics, but replaces the concealed literary references of Goethe's original with a more central literary theme. Haman the villain is now a poor poet for whom the Jewish threat is a threat from those who have not just an invisible God but also a love of real poetry, and he warns the king:

Ein wohlgefügter Staat kann eher Krieg und Schulden
Als einen Hauch von Kunst und gar von Dichtkunst
dulden.

In the third and final act, wholly missing in Goethe's original, Hacks, besides bringing the Esther-play to a happy end, develops the literary angle into a full-scale confrontation between rationalism and sentimentalism. In avoiding more overtly topical disputes Hacks, it might be said, risks archaism. His most obvious measure against that risk is perhaps his reduction of Goethe's original twenty-five characters to eighteen, who are to be performed by a maximum of three actors. The result, besides emphasizing the element of play-acting, is a step towards an anti-mimetic idiom of a more modern kind. But Hacks seems to rely most of all on an audience capable of supplying the twentieth-century dimension to eighteenth-century mannerisms. Thus, when Dörte Schievelbusch, daughter of the Magister, a dictatorial arbiter of taste, sings her *Vernunftreiche Gartenentzückung,* she praises, with the hungry in mind, edible vegetables, beginning with 'Die Kartoffel auch ist eine Blume'. In the bathos are exposed the pretensions of those who update a convention in the interests of a kind of 'Gebrauchslyrik'. When her Father, sworn devotee of the classical heritage, recites one of her own poems, 'Ausflug mit Aphrodite, oder: Herzerquickende Morgen-, Mittags-und Abendstunden', his lack of even imitative talent is obvious; less obvious perhaps is the possibility that Hacks may have later classicizing postures in mind:

Pirol lässt sein Lied ertönen
Und ich gehe mit der schönen

Aphrodite, ihre Hand
In der meinen, über Land.
Weg und Flur im Morgenscheine.
Vor uns her am Ackerraine
Wandelt eine Wachtel, die
Man nicht sieht, doch hört man sie.

At such points what Hacks adds to Goethe — and there is no such scene in Goethe's original — stays playfully close to the idiom of Goethe's fragment, seeming to build on the meanings which are there already.

For Hacks, to judge from his version of the *Jahrmarktsfest,* overhauling Goethe can involve rediscovering what has been forgotten rather than radically refashioning what is well known. Brecht, too, we remember, had made his own discoveries, reading *Der Sammler,* praising *Pandora.* This latter, the second of Hacks's adaptations, is more familiar than the *Jahrmarktsfest zu Plundersweilern,* but it is not a work commonly invoked in recent socialist discussions about the relevance of Goethe. Hacks is clear, if characteristically provocative, on this point: *Pandora* is, he claims in a lengthy essay which he appends to his text, 'kaum gelesen und nie aufgeführt. Das Stück darf für vollkommen unbekannt gelten'.

The play is part of no socialist canon, but in turning to it Hacks is, nevertheless, venturing on that richest of all strands of socialist tradition — the Promethean. In *Pandora* Prometheus has grown more practical of purpose than his 'Sturm und Drang' counterpart, enjoining his workers:

Erhebt die starken Arme leicht, dass taktbewegt
Ein kräft'ger Hämmerchortanz, laut erschallend, rasch
Uns das Geschmolzne vielfach strecke zum Gebrauch.

(lines 165-7)

More important still, he confronts in his brother Epimetheus a mode of being, of loving, of awaiting Pandora's return in fact, which challenges him in a way unimagined by the young Goethe. To attempt to complete the *Pandora*-fragment is to be unintimidated indeed. Again Hacks half adopts Goethe's idiom, but, because the original is grander, less racy, he risks yet greater archaisms than in his pastiche extension of the *Jahrmarktsfest.* Hacks has produced a complex hybrid in which he tests — and it is a daunting test — our recollection of Goethe's text. Thus, to give one of countless examples, Hacks's Epimetheus remembers his total trust in Pandora with two lines from Goethe (116-7) and three words — the final words — from Hacks:

> Vergebens rauchgebildet wünschenswerter Trug,
> Du trügst mich nicht, Pandora, mir die Einzige.
> Sie trog mich.

Our hearing is, of course, being tested, our capacity to catch either the inflexions and locutions of a later age or, when the register is deceptively close to Goethe, a shift towards the matter-of-fact which is out of key with Goethe's original. In the second part, at a stage where there is no equivalent scene in Goethe, Phileros, Prometheus's son, rejects wife, father and the society of man. The language harks back, but only partially, coming to rest, as it were, somewhere between Goethe's world and Hacks's.

> Es ist eine ekle Albernheit,
> Mit einem Weib sich anzubinden zu nem Paar
> Oder mit vielen Menschen klettend zum Verein . . .

But when he leaves he strikes a note coarser than any in Goethe's 'Festspiel':

> Ich gehe dann. Wie überlang vermisst ich das,
> Eine Zigarre und, wohin du schaust, kein Weib.

It is this ambiguously pitched diction which is Hacks's most obvious instrument in his adaptation of *Pandora*. By this means he effects changes of direction with few startling changes of idiom Phileros, for example, finds his father and the Titans wanting. The manner is convolutedly unmodern, the matter less so — the Promethean tradition is again under scrutiny:

> Wo andre den Titanen sehen, sehe ich
> Den eitlen Greis, schon glättet sich das Borstige,
> Denn nichts ist leichter täuschbar als gefühlter Wert.

Hacks indeed ultimately rejects Prometheus, presenting in Pandora herself, who returns as the play ends, the apotheosis of work wedded to feeling rather than divorced from it. Prometheus, somewhat dourly, yields the future to his brother:

> Nicht unstolz auf Vergangnes, schlag ich Künftges aus.
> Das Angenehme, meine Sache war es nie.

With the operatic close of Hacks's *Pandora* a different Goethe has, perhaps uncomfortably, been reinstated, the Goethe of the 'Festspiel'. Not a crypto-socialist Goethe, but, in Hacks's view, a Goethe relevant to socialist goals, goals which need no longer slavishly promote the Promethean. The play offers, as Hacks cryptically puts it, a 'Utopie der Kapsel und des Schreins', a stage, in other words, beyond technology. We are worlds away from Braun's astronaut, even farther perhaps from Plenzdorf's apprentice grappling with *Werther* in a lavatory.

Hacks's defence of Goethe against what he sees as the depredations of modernizers has yielded a different kind of play, written in the years between the *Jahrmarktsfest* and *Pandora*, which develops most strikingly the quest for authenticity which underlies both those adaptations. That play is *Ein Gespräch im Hause Stein über den abwesenden Herrn von Goethe*. Goethe, as Hacks has pointed out, is in the play — 'Gewiss kommt er vor, er tritt nur nicht auf'. Herr Stein, on the other hand, 'tritt auf und kommt nicht vor' — he is a stuffed figure in a chair. Only Charlotte von Stein has visible dramatic life, and that life is sustained, so to speak, by the absent Goethe. Goethe has, indeed, supplied Hacks with his starting-point. The date is October 1786; Goethe has left Weimar; Frau von Stein has no idea of his whereabouts. He was, of course, to reach Rome, via Venice, on 29 October; and the play ends with the arrival of his letter from Venice, written on 14 October.

Hacks owes more to Goethe than the bare chronology of his departure for Italy. Towards the end of 1786 and into 1787 Goethe's letters record an absence of letters from Frau von Stein. On 8/9 December he receives a mere 'Zettelgen' from her, on 13/16 December he records his pain at it — 'Du willst mir schweigen?' he asks. On 23 December he receives a letter full of 'schmerzliches', on 6 January a 'bitter süssen Brief'. Hacks has worked back from the recorded silences to the causes, and he finds them not in any pique at Goethe's disappearance but in the fact, sensed but not articulated by Frau von Stein at the end of the play, that she has totally failed to understand Goethe.

The temptation to see the play as the portrayal of an individual predicament is great, since the shape of the play, its climaxes and its pace, are so dependent on the shifting pattern of Charlotte's recollections, her suppressions and her half-admitted emotional crises. It is equally tempting to see the play as a skilfully documented interpretation of a unique relationship — Hacks knows the source-material, knows the poems sent in manuscript to Charlotte, knows the clues in Goethe's letters over ten years to the content of letters sent by her to him and lost. But the play has yet another more topical dimension. Hacks, it might be said, is overhauling not Goethe's work but our picture of him. He engages two targets at once and does so by both accepting and rejecting Frau von Stein's evidence. Goethe, we are told early in the play — or, rather, her stuffed husband is told — was a 'Grobian': 'Er war berühmt und ein Grobian: er war vielleicht der berühmteste Grobian in den deutschen Staaten'. He was unkempt, his hair uncombed and he was given immoderately to drinking Franconian wine:

> Seine Backen röten sich und zeigen hässliche Adern, die Augen sind verschwollen, das gedunsene Gesicht zergeht in unedle Falten, und er redet mit schleppender Zunge.

Frau von Stein, unintimidated by talk of genius, is correcting a romanticized picture, restoring the warts and the scruffiness. But if we applaud the note of realism, we do not applaud the general response to Goethe of which it is a part. She has her own preconceptions about how a poet should act, look and talk (for the foul-mouthed Goethe, she archly notes, 'Guten Morgen' was 'minder natürlich als Schlag der Donner drein'); and they are essentially philistine preconceptions, because she insists that the poet practise what she thinks he preaches. Nor is poetry itself an excuse for bad manners, since it is peripheral: 'Nun ist er am Ende wieder zur Schriftstellerei zurückgekehrt, also nichts geworden. Schliesslich Schriftsteller, das ist kein Beruf.'

Charlotte is likewise dismissive about her own influence over Goethe. He, we remember, had put that influence in unforgotten words ('Tropftest Mässigung dem heissen Blute . . .'). She puts it differently: 'Er war ein Lump; ich erzog ihn; jetzt haben wir einen erzogenen Lumpen: ein Genie'. And at another point Goethe's poem is put in its place: 'Nichts gegen die tiefen Blicke, das zärtliche Gestammel', she laconically observes, but 'irgendwann muss ja auch eine ernsthaftere Erörterung folgen'. The nagging is part of an attempt to tame a power which she cannot grasp, and in making the attempt she displays not only her philistinism but also her reactionary instincts. Defending the status quo against Goethe's mildly egalitarian tax-schemes means defending inherited wealth 'gegen den Neid des Pöbels'. 'Und ich sagte zu Goethe', she recollects, 'Geduld, mein junger Freund, der Fortschritt kommt bestimmt, und ich bin überaus froh, dort zu leben, wo er nicht kommt.'

In all this Hacks works obliquely — Goethe, after all, does not appear, but Frau von Stein's nitpicking incomprehension is counterproductive, enhancing him and diminishing her, re-establishing the distance between her kind of bourgeois society and Goethe. The Goethe who defies her trivializing critique is certainly not the socialist Goethe-Prometheus reborn, nor Goethe-Orest, 'geheilt und entsühnt', in the words of Erich Trunz, under Frau von Stein's influence. Indeed Hacks, chary of labels, seems to be restoring to Goethe a degree of masterful inscrutability. The result is however, not an old icon dusted down and put back, but Goethe and Goethe reception scrutinized in modern terms; and this is due not least to the effect of Charlotte von Stein's language. She inhabits two dimensions of time — her quaint formalities smack of an earlier age, but her racy, no-nonsense manner has a more contemporary ring. The implication is clear: confused, opinionated, philistine grappling with Goethe did not cease with Frau von Stein in the autumn of 1786.

'Die Einschüchterung durch Klassizität war durchbrochen. Würde und Humor fanden sich in gutem Verhältnis.' The words might be a verdict on the efforts of the three writers, Brecht, Braun and Hacks, in their various encounters with Goethe. In fact they are not. They introduce an article on four current East German *Faust* productions, which appeared in the East German cultural weekly *Sonntag* in its issue of 28 February 1982. Clearly the problem diagnosed by Brecht in that essay of 1954 has persisted. Clearly too the problem has been for many a creative opportunity, and one of those who seized the opportunity—Volker Braun—has given what could be said to be a résumé of why it is important to be unintimidated. In 1968 he wrote a short piece entitled 'Die Goethepächter', which is worth quoting in full as a conclusion to my argument, since it returns the efforts of Braun and others to their context, reminding us that they were making those efforts in order to keep Goethe truly alive in the face of those who had solemnly nominated themselves the sole guardians of the Goethe inheritance:

Die Goethepächter

Sie haben aus Goethes Werk einen Werkhof gemacht für

die schwer erziehbare Nation. Sie schalten darin wie Gouvernanten. Wie wenig Liebe zum Heutigen spür ich in ihrem Gehabe.

Sie haben sein Erbe gepachtet und bleiben darin sitzen. Sie haben seine Schwellen gebohnert —aber wagen sich nicht mehr darüber. Sie leben mit seinen Büchern so, als würden die Bücher schon leben. Sie haben so mit ihnen zu tun, als hätten sie nichts mit sich zu tun.

Während wir, auf den Wiesen der öffentlichen Landschaft, mit ihm unsre Spässe treiben. Sie sind neue Aristokraten; wir sind seine alten Freunde.

Notes to On not being Intimidated: Socialist Overhauling of a Classic

1. The phases of the debate, with summaries of the many colloquia devoted to the subject, have been recorded — and, indeed, on occasion initiated — by the journal *Weimarer Beiträge*. A recent West German survey is Wolfram Schlenker, *Das 'kulturelle Erbe' in der DDR: Gesellschaftliche Entwicklung und Kulturpolitik 1945-1965* (Stuttgart, 1977). Schlenker, whose concluding summary traces developments as far as the mid-1970s, finds no evidence of change in official attitudes to the heritage in general, Goethe and Schiller in particular. A contrary view, adducing evidence of change, is advanced in an East German essay: Hans Kaufmann, *Versuch über das Erbe* (Leipzig, 1980).

2. Wekwerth's documentation of the *Urfaust* production has been published in Manfred Wekwerth, *Schriften: Arbeit mit Brecht* (Berlin, 1975), pp. 99 ff. Brecht's own notes, along with his essay, are in *Gesammelte Werke* (Frankfurt am Main, 1967), XVII, 1275 ff. Parts of the *Urfaust* production were filmed — with a fixed, 8 mm camera — by H. Jürgen Syberberg and included in his film of the Berliner Ensemble, *Nach meinem letzten Umzug*. In his commentary in the film Hans Mayer emphasizes the boldness of Brecht's conception.

3.   Ulbricht's attack was directed against both Brecht's *Urfaust* and Hanns Eisler's *Johann Faustus*. The latter was planned as an opera, but only the libretto was written. It was revised, with help from Brecht, and published in 1952. It is in no sense a version of Goethe, but Eisler's radical re-treatment of the historical Faust and Brecht's commitment to it in his 'Thesen zur Faustus-Diskussion' (*Gesammelte Werke,* XIX, 533 ff.) suggest that the attack on 'Einschüchterung' can in some degree be seen as a joint venture.

4.   The leading satirical-cultural journal *Süddeutscher Postillon* devoted its birthday-number (Nr. 17, 1899) to 'Goethe-Prometheus'. On the role of Goethe's poem see Peter Müller, 'Goethes "Prometheus": Sinn- und Urbild bürger-lichen Emanzipationsanspruchs', *Weimarer Beiträge,* 22 (1976), Heft 3, 52-82.

5.   On the debate and the general context of East German *Werther*-reception see J. Scharfschwerdt, 'Werther in der DDR. Bürgerliches Erbe zwischen sozialistischer Kulturpolitik und gesellschaftlicher Realität', *Jahrbuch der deutschen Schiller-gesellschaft,* 22 (1978), 235-76.

Last Universal Man — or Wilful Amateur? On the Claims made for his Natural Philosophy R.H. Stephenson

The many-sided nature of Goethe's activity has inevitably attracted the label of Universal Man. He seems to rank with Aristotle and Leonardo both in the breadth of his interests and in the enthusiastic commitment he brought to them. Not only was he poet, prose-writer and playwright of stupendous variety of style; he also spent a great deal of his time immersed in the practice and theory of the plastic arts, in the observation of nature in every kind of manifestation (while reflecting all the while on the methodological problems involved), in running various departments of the government of Saxe-Weimar, including the onerous one of theatre-management. However, those who use the tag are faced with the, at first sight, perplexing fact that he was, at the same time, an untiring advocate of the advantages of specialization. 'Your general culture is all nonsense' he has his spokesman, Jarno, say in *Wilhelm Meisters Wanderjahre* (HA, VIII, 282),[1] thus offering to posterity one of his many provoking correctives to any easy assimilation of his own vision of wholeness to the more traditional, and simpler, views of what constitutes a Whole Man that we tend to associate with the Greeks and the Renaissance. Moreover, if those who hail him as a *Universalgenie* have no more in mind than the range of his interests, then all that is needed to deflate the implicit challenge, so irksome to us distracted and over-specialized citizens of the twentieth century, is the historical evidence: most of the subjects which attracted Goethe's attention were, seen from our perspective, strikingly underdeveloped. Boerhaave, for instance, (on whom Goethe drew for much of his self-tuition in science) was simultaneously professor of botany, chemistry, medicine and pharmacology, any one of which would require the provision of at least two — if not more! — chairs in a modern university. From some quarters, indeed — in particular from nineteenth-century positivists impressed by the ever-growing wealth of data that needs to be mastered in even the most limited area of a science — has come the charge of dilettantism, of 'wertlose und totgeborene Spielerei' (Du Bois-Reymond). And despite the profound respect which — among other modern, and methodologically more sophisticated, scientists — Werner Heisenberg and Max Planck have shown for the accuracy and suggestiveness of Goethe's scientific studies, the charge still retains some force. If only because, operating with so problematic a notion of universality, scholarly defences of Goethe too often sound like special pleading. But, here again, disquieting facts stand in the way of simply exchanging one label for another and of regarding the large number of non-literary works as dabblings of mere biographical-historical value. For it is generally acknowledged that Goethe made significant discoveries in his scientific work; and he has been cited by reputable authorities as the conceptual father of several developments in various fields. The problems posed by an evaluation of Goethe's manifold activities are clearly related to a wider issue, over which we still agonize 150 years after his death: namely the proper relation, at all levels of education, between 'breadth' and 'depth', between 'liberal culture' and 'specialization'. And it is in this respect, as in so many others, that his example remains an instructive inspiration.

Perhaps one reason for our inability to solve this central question is that we do not distinguish as carefully as Goethe himself did between the negative and positive aspects of amateurism, between the dilettante on the one hand and the amateur on the other. With a precision born of the painful, personal experience of trying to integrate the often conflicting tendencies of his own rich endowment, Goethe recorded in his essays, letters, diaries, and (often most revealingly) in his unpublished notes, from his early Frankfurt days on, a high estimation of the *Liebhaber* proper, while denigrating the complementary negative figure, the *Dilettant* — a subtle and sophisticated distinction that contains, as Georg Simmel pointed out, the germ of Goethe's outlook on culture. In following up this insight of Simmel's, Hans R. Vaget, in his

Dilettantismus und Meisterschaft (Munich, 1971), has, by piecing together the evidence, provided a most useful exposition of Goethe's views on dilettantism. An avowedly genetic method, however, leads him to neglect conceptual analysis in favour of speculative, psycho-biographical explanations of what he regards as occasional blurrings and 'discontinuities' in Goethe's thinking (see pp. 77, 143, and especially, 210). Notwithstanding Goethe's rhetorical use of the key-*terms,* 'Liebhaber', 'Dilettant' and their cognates (now in a negative, now in a positive sense), the *concepts* are, to my mind, always kept clearly and logically distinct. Both dilettante and amateur lack in Goethe's account that special aptitude that enables the professional to *master* his chosen field; but there the similarity ends. The dilettante is a variant of that psychological type the eighteenth century never tired of denouncing, the Enthusiast. His experience of the activity he would practise is at fault because his theorizing about it is flawed — and flawed precisely because it is not grounded in experience. At bottom, the dilettante and amateur lack in Goethe's account that special tact, flexibility, and courage to move, as appropriate, from theory to practice and back again. The inevitable result is a still-born *Pfuscherei,* a botching marked by either pedantry (technique without significance) or incompetence (fervour without form). A tendency to make excuses and an indulgence of mediocrity — 'Nichts ist dem Dilettanten mehr entgegen als feste Grundsätze und strenge Anwendung derselben' ('Über strenge Urteile'; WA, i, XLVII, 49) — are the consequences of the self-deception and solipsism essential to sustaining such uncreative work, far outweighing any possible gains in terms of the cultivation of one's faculties or the dissemination of a general 'refinement'. It is in the 'Walpurgisnachtstraum' of his *Faust* that Goethe presents a whole array of variations on such dilettantism, each of which is characterized by sexual substitutionalism, a quick and impatient marrying of high and low, flesh and spirit, theory and practice (symbolically represented in the scene by Ariel and Puck respectively). The result is immediate gratification, but pretentious and empty productions such as the soap-bubble bagpipe that never takes off — a satire on bungling that passes itself off as art:

> Kleiner Schritt und hoher Sprung
> Durch Honigtau und Düfte

Zwar du trippelst mir genung,
Doch geht's nicht in die Lüfte.   (lines 4263-6)

By contrast, the amateur is well aware of his own limitations. Conscious that the master's superiority —unattainable save by a pupil of comparable potential —consists in an ability, not simply to relate, but to correlate theory and practice, intellectual and mechanical expertise, to such a degree 'dass man auf diesen höheren Stufen nicht wissen kann, sondern tun muss; so wie an einem Spiele wenig zu wissen und alles zu leisten ist' (*Maximen und Reflexionen*, edited Hecker, no. 419), the amateur is content to view the master as a purely regulative model: he learns, like any good student, one aspect of his chosen activity after another, step by step, all the while seriously endeavouring to understand, and then carry out, the techniques involved. The fruits of his labour, though inevitably inferior to the expert's, have considerable value nonetheless: they serve him, and may well serve others, as aids to understanding the significance of more accomplished work. The amateur's aim, then, is not the dilettante's of deceiving himself, and possibly others, by passing himself off as a professional *manqué*. The amateur's principal purpose is to achieve such competence as he can so that he may enjoy and evaluate, to the best of his ability, the results arrived at by professional practitioners.

Nothing illustrates better Goethe's conscientious observance of these ground-rules than his scientific endeavours. He preferred to call himself a *Naturschauer* (an 'observer of nature') rather than a *Naturforscher* (an 'investigator of nature'), and for very good reason. In a remarkably candid little piece, entitled 'Self-description', of 1797 he stated that 'he did not have sufficient perseverance' for the sciences (HA, X, 529). What exactly he meant by that is clear from other statements that he makes about his own limitations. He was well aware that a master-scientist must be able to sustain thought at a high level of abstraction in order to produce testable, explanatory theories — the professional physicist, he says in his *Farbenlehre* (HA, XIII, 482-3) must be a mathematician, and something of a philosopher too. He never made any secret of the fact that he was no mathematician himself, telling his friend, Zelter, on one occasion that no-one could be more wary of numbers than he (in a letter, 12 December 1812; compare *Zur Farbenlehre,* HA, XIII, 483-4); and in an essay devoted to outlining his indebtedness to Kant he began with the famous words: 'Für Philosophie im eigentlichen Sinne hatte ich kein Organ' ('Einwirkung der neueren Philosophie'). Equally restricting was the fact, as he told Eckermann on 1 February 1827, that instruments of magnification were not compatible with his own modes of observation. But, despite these limitations, there is not a hint in any of his statements on theorizing, mathematics, or the use of scientific instruments of the kind of defensive, anti-scientific rancour that might have been fostered by a dilettante's inferiority complex vis-à-vis those endowed with gifts he lacked. His acceptance of theory is whole-hearted; not for him any naive belief in immaculate perception! Even in his 'Sturm und Drang' days, when attacking what he considered to be a false aesthetic theory, he indicated the value of 'wahre Theorie', i.e., of one properly related to practice ('Sulzer-Rezension'; HA, XII, 19); and in a much later essay, 'Analyse und Synthese' of 1829, he attacked as the worst possible error that of analysing without a theory about what the whole is that is being analysed. Clearly, his inability to *produce* theory did not inhibit him from *using* theories, as *modi cognoscendi,* for the purposes of clarification. He borrowed freely from others, as H.B. Nisbet's book on *Goethe and the Scientific Tradition* has persuasively demonstrated; but always, as in his *Metamorphose der Pflanzen,* subordinating what he took to his own distinctive purpose. Nor did he feel any need to disparage mathematics. On the contrary, he told Eckermann (20 December 1826) he considered it 'the most sublime and useful science', a sentiment he published in an essay written in the same year ('Uber Mathematik und deren Missbrauch'; WA, ii, XI, 78-95), in which he deplored his reputation as an opponent of a subject that 'no one can hold in higher esteem'. His one contention with regard to mathematics (*about* which he knew a good deal) was not that it was inapplicable to the physical world, as some commentators would have it; but the ancient view, reinforced by Galileo's distinction between the quantitative and the qualitative, that the quantifying methods of mathematics were out of place for some aspects of nature. Indeed there were, he felt, certain parts of his own *Farbenlehre* which would benefit from mathematical treatment (HA, XIII, 484). Similarly his well-known utterances on the use of instruments are often quoted only to mislead. When he says that 'microscopes and telescopes in fact confuse pure common sense'

(Hecker, no. 502), he is merely repeating a commonplace that came into currency at the time of the acception of the microscope, whose use had led to the survival of the wrong-headed 'preformation' theory of biological development. The point he is endorsing is the one made by Democritus in insisting on the distortions caused by any kind of mediation in perception. Goethe is not *condemning* technological advances — he had, after all, praised Herschel's use of the telescope in the same conversation in which he confessed his own inability to exploit such instruments. He is simply recommending due caution.

These are hardly the views of a man 'in opposition to modern science'. The complexity of Goethe's outlook simply does not conform to the image that has been foisted on him in the twentieth century by scholars who would make him over into a champion of their own, often ill-informed, fears of what they think science is about. No one lacking deep sympathy with the aims and methods of science could have written the exquisite poem, 'Herbstgefühl':

> Fetter grüne, du Laub
> Das Rebengeländer
> Hier mein Fenster herauf.
> Gedrängter quillet,
> Zwillingsbeeren, und reifet
> Schneller und glänzend voller.
> Euch brütet der Mutter Sonne
> Scheideblick, euch umsäuselt
> Des holden Himmels
> Feuchtende Fülle.
> Euch kühlet des Monds
> Freundlicher Zauberhauch,
> Und euch betauen, ach,
> Aus diesen Augen
> Der ewig belebenden Liebe
> Voll schwellende Tränen.

For here the feelings attendant on an interventionist and exploitative attitude to nature are given aesthetic expression. Man, distanced from nature (there is a window between the speaker and the external world) and indifferent to its specific detail (the individual grapes are described as 'twins'), is struggling to make it meet man-made standards (a process embodied in the clenched control of the syntax in the first six lines as in the reiteration of comparatives), in order to produce something that is at once an intensification of nature's processes and a delight to man — wine.

Goethe's statements on modern science are those of a man who, while aware of his own limitations, is confident of possessing certain gifts that enable him to make a worthwhile contribution to a field of endeavour the importance of which he never doubts. And his gifts and his interests are reciprocally related. A sensitivity that enabled him to perceive the finest detail, a methodical mind that constructed well-organized and meticulously recorded experiments, and a lively intellect that empowered him to entertain, and where necessary to integrate, various available theories, all combined to direct his attention to what he called the 'incommensurable' aspects of nature. What caught Goethe's interest was the form and function of phenomena in their fully concrete individuality; his aim was to penetrate into the specific self-regulation that inheres in all organisms. The success he achieved in this endeavour was, he felt, not due to his possessing any extraordinary gifts, but rather to the systematic nature of his efforts — 'ein folgerechtes Bemühen'. Gifts he shared with many another were intensified to the point where they combined into a fine art; and it is the record he left of this systematized amateurism that constitutes the continuing relevance of his scientific activity.

The first step is one of systematic comparison, a mode of thought that came naturally enough to an adherent of a metaphysic postulating a Great Chain of Being. As a preliminary Goethe is happy to use available theories about the phenomena he wishes to examine: sometimes those we call 'common sense'; often two or more theories that are conceptually incompatible. His purpose at this point is not coherent explanation but merely the illumination of as many perceptible details as possible in order to familiarize himself with the objects under scrutiny — for which purpose he himself kept large collections of natural phenomena: 'mit Ordnung zu wissen, erfordert genaue Kenntnis der einzelnen Gegenstände' (WA, ii, VI, 300). Naive induction he rejected as firmly as ever Hume did —'Induktion ist bloss demjenigen nütze der überreden will' (WA, ii, XI, 309). Instead he uses cautious, theory-laden analogy, comparing objects on the basis of partial similarities of structure until enough of these similarities are noted in a number of phenomena to posit with a degree of probability what he calls a 'virtual identity' between them ('eine virtuelle Gleichheit'; WA, ii, VI, 287). As his formulation implies, Goethe is quite aware that this is a concept and not a reality — 'eine Art von Ideal', as he puts it in 'Erfahrung und Wissenschaft'. What we actually perceive are best thought of as variations on this *Typus*. Its value lies in its providing the mind with a constant — the same relative position, in all variations of a type, of their shared elements — and one that, while open to modification in the light of further experience, serves two essential purposes in Goethe's quest for organized knowledge: 1) to facilitate any further comparisons which newly discovered phenomena may call for; and 2) to regulate the next step in his procedure, that of experimentation.

In a finely drawn essay written in 1792 entitled 'Experiment as Mediator between Object and Subject', Goethe outlined his position in respect of experimentation. He is as critical as are present-day philosophers of science of the practice of trying to *prove* theories by means of experiments; as he insisted in conversation with Eckermann (1 February 1827), the most crucial are those that have the potential to *refute* the theory being tested. And when he reformulates, in one of his maxims (Hecker, no. 115), Bacon's point that experiments that are carefully designed to exclude side-effects are a kind of 'torture' of nature in order to get a clear-cut yes-or-no answer about the adequacy of a theory, his statement, like those he makes on the use of scientific instruments, is corrective, not dismissive, in intent. His interest however lies, naturally enough as an amateur scientist lacking the ability to conceive original theories, not in testing a theory, not primarily in what he calls the 'wissenschaftliches Phänomen', but, like Bacon's, in increasing his knowledge of the living phenomenon in all its given contingency. His aim is to make sense of the process of change that underlies those variations which the employment of a Type has brought to light. He first observes the phenomenon in its immediate environment, in the 'basis of its existence', noting its relations with other forms. In order to study the dynamics of this complex he *imagines* it as a successive series in time, each stage imaginatively derived (*abgeleitet* is his term), extending backwards (and sometimes forward) from a 'pregnant point' at which the complexity of interrelations reaches its highest degree of intricacy.

Regulating the close observation of each 'stage' of this series is the Type-concept derived from the earlier comparative studies; and the goal of this Goethean experimentation is what he most often refers to as an *Idee,* a construct as essentially mental as the *Typus,* given birth in the memory:

> When, having something before me that has grown, I inquire after its genesis and measure the process as far back as I can, I become aware of a series of stages that, though I cannot actually see them in succession, I can present to myself in memory as *a kind of ideal whole.*
>
> (WA, ii, VI, 303-4; my italics)

By sticking so close to the object in its setting — the whole complex is regarded as if it were 'one big phenomenon' (WA, ii, XI, 44) — Goethe seeks to avoid any arbitrary connections the imagination might be tempted to establish: in his experiments the faculty of memory has the dominant role. The resultant synthesis, reflecting a natural progression — 'der Beobachter muss mehr das Ordnen als das Verbinden und Knüpfen lieben' (ibid., 43) — is the Archetype proper, a model embracing both the static Type-concept *and* a mental picture of the phenomenon's growth-pattern, the metamorphosis of its basic form.

Unlike the simpler concept of a Type, the Archetype (the best-known example of which is the *Urpflanze*, the 'basic plant') cannot be adequately expressed in purely denotative language, since it embraces both simultaneity and succession:

> For strictly speaking we try in vain to express the essence of a thing. All that we can become aware of are effects, and a complete history of such effects would presumably at least approximate to the essence of that same thing.
>
> ('Vorwort zur Farbenlehre')

Such processes, as he told Hegel in his letter of 7 October 1820, on the occasion of the latter's enthusiastic response to his essay on entoptic phenomena, are difficult to express in words because they are in essence visual phenomena. But despite the fact, so much admired by modern scientists, that Goethe's experiments *are* repeatable; and despite his recommendation that a few of his simpler experiments in chromatics might, for illustrative purposes, be repeated by his readers (*Zur Farbenlehre*; HA, XIII, 396), it would be a mistake to suppose that he regards repetition as necessary, or in most cases even desirable. Rather than engage in such inefficient activities, which run the risk of becoming unthinking, naively empiricist, imitations (WA, ii, XI, 271), the reader is encouraged by Goethe's highly sophisticated employment of a metaphorical language based on a figurative use of the simplest operations of nature, such as polarity — a mode of expression that presupposes some 'genuine perception' (*Zur Farbenlehre*; HA, XIII, 488-93) — to 'see' with his mind's eye what the experimenter observes with his physical eye:

> If [a book that deals with natural phenomena] is to be enjoyed, if it is to be used, then nature must be present to the reader either in reality or in vivid imagination.
>
> (HA, XIII, 321)

By means of what he calls a 'naturgemässe Darstellung' — a vivid presentation of a series of experiments — the reader is enabled to store the impressions thus gained, in his own memory, until they yield for him what they yield for the experimental observer: the 'idea' of the metamorphosis of the phenomenon in question.

Equipped with these powerful abstractions — the products, as Goethe has it, of the 'self-rectifying operations of common sense' — the amateur scientist is now able, like the professional armed with the sophisticated abstractions of mathematics, to match theory with perception, in the hope of gaining that deep insight into the workings of nature which, as Arthur Koestler and others have convincingly argued, lies at the root of all great scientific discoveries. Profound insight of this kind, accompanied by an overwhelming sense of conviction, is what Goethe experienced when he matched his intellectual construct of a basic plant, 'eine übersinnliche Urpflanze', with sensuously apprehended plants 'unter der sinnlichen Form' ('Geschichte meiner botanischen Studien'; HA, XIII, 164). There is none of the epistemological naivety that is sometimes attributed to it in this transition from sense-perception through concept to the higher percept that he called *Anschauung*. He was far too schooled in Kant ever to seek to know the thing-in-itself, the elemental world totally unstructured by the human mind. In the Introduction to his *Farbenlehre* he expressed the hope that philosophers would be pleased that he had not ventured beyond the phenomenological world; 'dass wir gesucht die Phänomene bis zu ihren Urquellen zu verfolgen, bis dorthin, wo sie bloss *erscheinen und sind* . . . ' (HA, XIII, 327; my italics). But he does think that it is true to the spirit, if not to the letter, of Kant's epistemology to postulate a mode of perception — called, in the essay devoted to the topic, 'Anschauende Urteilskraft' — which, though operating with abstractions, is nonetheless firmly grounded in sensuous experience. He referred to the faculty necessary for such perception as 'the highest reason' (Eckermann, 13 February 1829); by which he meant a slight extension of Kant's notion of an *intellectus archetypus,* an intellect which moves from whole to parts and which Kant had attributed to the divine. Goethe posits just such a regulative faculty at work in man, co-ordinating all his other faculties (including 'reason' in its usual sense), and enabling man to 'participate intellectually in nature's productions':

> Here the phenomenon of the after-image, memory, productive imagination, concept, and idea must all be in play at once, and be manifest in the living organ of perception, with complete freedom, and without purpose or guidance.
>
> (WA, ii, XI, 283)

By *Nachbild*, 'after image', he means the sense-trace, or sense-memory, left in our organs of perception. And the seat of this 'free-play' of all our faculties is what he once called the 'exact sensory imagination' ('exakte sinnliche Phantasie'; HA, XIII, 42). The imagination — whose normal function (in the Kantian scheme Goethe is working with) is the application of concepts derived from the understanding on to sense-impressions — is here given a secondary function, one in which mental entities and sense-impressions play an equal role.

Goethe's favoured term for the object of this higher perception is *das Urphänomen*, by which he distinguishes it from both the phenomenon uncovered by the inevitable distortions of all kinds of experimentation and from that construed by everyday common sense ('das empirische Phänomen'). It is in this sense that he can endorse the Platonic view that sense-perception can distort truth: 'what we find so confusing when we seek to recognize the idea in the phenomenal world is that it often, indeed usually, contradicts our senses' (Hecker, no. 1138). It is, he notes, obvious that this higher mode of perception is very close to that of an artist

(HA, XIII, 55). Just as an artist co-ordinates abstract forms, borrowed or invented, with what might best be called the 'contours' of his chosen medium, in order to yield a new form, the work of art; so too, the *Naturschauer*, intent on seeing into the life of things, matches whatever heuristic intellectual forms he has available with the welter of concrete detail his sensibility exposes him to. And just as, for instance, discursive relations are transformed in what Goethe called the 'veil of poetry' by such sensuously apprehended features as rhythm and rhyme; so too, our pre-conceived ideas about a phenomenon are subtly 'corrected' by our sensitivity to sensuous patterns inhering in the phenomenon itself. If Goethe insists that the 'idea manifest in appearance' is a true 'revelation', an *Offenbarung*, it is because the objectivity of this 'pure phenomenon' is phenomenologically guaranteed by the fact that what is perceived is a *self*-regulation at work between the sensuous elements in the object. (He is well aware that these elements are 'taken' from the world by our apprehension.) The result is a sensuously apprehended form embodied in the objects so lovingly contemplated:

> A drive to perceive living structures as such has emerged at all times, even in men of science — a drive to grasp the external, visible, palpable parts as a whole, to construe them as indications of what is within, and so to master, to a certain extent, the whole in perception.   (ibid.)

Thus an *Urphänomen* like the magnet may 'reveal itself':

> *The pure phenomenon* is the final precipitate of all ex-periences and experiments. It can never be isolated, but rather *reveals itself* in a constant succession of manifestations.
> ('Erfahrung und Wissenschaft'; second italics mine)

And since the stages of comparison and experimentation (or some other means of achieving adequate abstraction) are pre-requisite to the aperçu of this self-sustaining and immanent 'law', Goethe on occasion identifies the whole mental process involved with the object perceived: 'Was ist eine höhere Synthese als ein lebendiges Wesen?' ('Analyse und Synthese'). To call such percep-tion 'aesthetic' is not to downgrade it so long as we bear in mind the very precise meaning Goethe, in consort with Schiller, gave to the term 'beauty': 'The beautiful is a *manifestation* of secret laws of nature, which would have remained for ever hidden from us but for this *appearance*' (Hecker, no.183; my italics). If we mean by beauty what Schiller meant when he defined it as 'Freiheit in der Erscheinung', i.e., the manifestation of self-regulation, then we may safely dub Goethe's *Anschauung* 'aesthetic perception'. In doing so we gain a precise understanding of what he held modern science must needs neglect: 'If, therefore, I say "this animal is beautiful", I would be wasting my time were I to try to prove the statement by means of some proportion of number or measure . . .'. For the quality of beauty inheres in a specific configuration of sense qualities for which there can be no substitute (HA, XIII, 21f.).

But for all his insistence that the mind of man cannot penetrate beyond the *Urphänomen*, Goethe does not hold the rather precious view that has been put into his mouth by many commentators, namely that man cannot, by means of theoretical abstraction, penetrate more deeply into it: 'There is a great difference between dimly apprehending with dull senses a vague whole and seeing and grasping acutely a complete whole' ('Einleitung in die Propyläen'; HA, XII, 51). What he sought to make clear was that he himself was not undertaking what he quite explicitly leaves to others better qualified than himself; viz. the elaboration of a theory which, though inevitably reductive, would yet be more adequate to the perceived phenomenon than any hitherto available: 'I always sought to master the simplest phenomenon and waited for elaboration from others' (WA, ii, XI, 301). There are, he says, minds stimulated by the excitement of the aperçu vouchsafed in *Anschauung*, that undertake the task of explaining what it is they have perceived:

> Perception (*Anschauen*) gives us at once the complete concept of an achieved form; the faculty of thought, not wishing to lag behind, shows and articulates in its own way how such a form could and must be achieved.
>
> ('Der Kammerberg bei Eger (1)'; HA, XIII, 268).

The fruit of this process, once the imagination takes a hand, is a new conceptual entity — a new scientific theory — that promises to sharpen our perception of its intuitive base:

> Since [the faculty of thought] does not feel entirely adequate to the task, it calls on the imagination for help;

and in this way such conceptual entities (*entia rationis*) gradually arise whose great advantage it is to lead us back to perception and to pressure us into greater attention and complete insight. (ibid.)

That is why he says that a physicist must not neglect philosophy; for the insight that marks the high-point of observation must become the starting point of philosophically sophisticated theorizing: ' [der Philosoph] nimmt aus des Physikers Hand ein Letztes, *das bei ihm ein Erstes wird*' (*Zur Farbenlehre*; HA, XIII, 483; my italics). It is here that amateur and professional part company. In much the same way as the born artist transmutes his perceptions into his chosen medium, the professional scientist has an aptitude for transposing his aperçus into theoretical terms. Lacking any such 'Organ' himself, Goethe modestly entitles his major scientific work, *Entwurf einer Farbenlehre*, a preparatory 'sketch' of a theory of colours; and he regrets that his lay-readers stray off into abstractions when they are better equipped for observation (Eckermann, 1 February 1827).

This is not, however, to say that the amateur has nothing to contribute directly to the professional sciences. The list of achievements attributed to Goethe — the discovery of the inter-maxillary bone in man; his theory of the genesis of the skull from the backbone, of plant metamorphosis; his founding of the science of morphology — which towards the end of his life brought him the recognition of leading scientists of the day, is a convincing answer to the question posed in the Concluding Remarks to his *Farbenlehre*: '. . . what can someone who is not in a position to devote his whole life to the sciences yet achieve and contribute to them?'. Moreover, the conceptual stimulation his scientific work has given later workers fully justifies his claim — couched for maximum rhetorical effect in the negative-sounding, and italicized, terms of dilettantism — that experience shows 'dass *Dilettanten* zum Vorteil der Wissenschaften vieles beitragen' ('Geschichte meiner botanischen Studien'; HA, XIII, 159). Fields as disparate as Gestalt-psychology and botany acknowledge his morphological method as an inspiration. But the most important aspect of amateur science does not lie in such spin-off benefits. It lies much more in the cultural value of properly conducted amateurism. The fact that the amateur and the professional cultivate different approaches to nature makes possible a serious dialogue which promises to bridge the gap between the so-called 'two cultures' far more effectively than the dilettantish dabblings glibly suggested in our own day. The amateur — unlike the dillettante who, lacking any grasp of method, is interested only in 'curiosities' and isolated facts — is in a position to appreciate and support the professional's endeavour, in much the same way as a music-lover supports his favourite art. Furthermore, he is also in a position — indeed it is his clear duty (see his letter to Zauper of 7 September 1821) — to differ when he thinks, as Goethe did in the case of Newton's *Opticks,* that the professional has made mistakes of reasoning and method, or, most important, is claiming too much for his theory.

Many of Goethe's criticisms of Newton's account of colour are methodological: he accuses him of unnecessary complication; of mistakes of interpretation; of occasional self-contradictions; and of making false predictions — all of which, to judge by the recent spate of critical works taken up in the new biography of Newton by R.S. Westfall (Cambridge, 1980), are wholly justified. But these errors are, for Goethe, symptomatic of a far graver flaw. When he told Eckermann (2 May 1824) that he regarded 'the Newtonian error' as his intellectual inheritance, he had in mind his contention that the phenomenon Newton sought to explain was merely an artificial construct, a 'scientific phenomenon', which Newton was passing off *as if it were an object of perception* ('Analyse und Synthese'). Broken light only yielded colour, held Goethe (rightly), under certain conditions, i.e., in an experimental situation (*Geschichte der Farbenlehre*; HA, XIV, 149). To mistake this for the living phenomenon of colour is to confound the derivative with the original (*Zur Farbenlehre*; HA, XIII, 482): 'dass Newton und seine Schule dasjenige mit Augen zu sehen glauben, was sie in die Phänomene hinein theorisiert haben, das ist es eben, worüber man sich beschwert' (WA, ii, II, 128). Not that Goethe thought that colour could not, or should not, be measured in terms of wave length; or that Newton's theory was not fruitful: Goethe accepts that his mathematical treatment of incidence is correct, and indeed predicts that Newton's results will be assimilable to any new theory based on his own preparatory findings ('Vorwort zur Farbenlehre'; HA, XIII, 319). His objection is not that Newton's theory is inadequate — that is true, more or less, of all theories. The point is a cultural rather than a narrowly scientific one:

Newton's manner of presentation will help displace our living perceptions of the world through the dead letter of abstractions ('Analyse und Synthese'). It is the 'hardening', by linguistic sleights of hand, of what are mere constructs into pseudo-realities that Goethe is protesting against. Disciplined by his poetic practice in an age unsurpassed for linguistic sophistication, Goethe was as sensitive as ever Whitehead was to 'the fallacy of misplaced concreteness': the interpolation between man and the living dynamic world of a distorting, grey, abstract schema. Reification is what the scientist must, at all costs, be on his guard against (*Zur Farbenlehre*; HA, XIII, 482). And it is the enlightened amateur's proper function to protest 'aus voller Kehle' whenever the scientist so forgets himself as to believe 'wenn man ein Gefolgertes ausgesprochen hatte, dass man den Gegenstand, die Erscheinung ausspreche' (*Geschichte der Farbenlehre*; HA, XIV, 137). Critics who are scandalized at the 'unprofessional' *ad hominem* tone of some of Goethe's strictures on Newton miss the point. It is not just that many of Goethe's remarks reveal a genuine reverence for a man he had no hesitation in ranking with the likes of Plato (HA, XIV, 143), or that he voices his admiration for Newton's strength of character in pursuing scholarship under most adverse circumstances (HA, XIV, 171). Nor is Goethe's personal critique fully explained by recalling the eighteenth-century idolatory of Newton with which any opponent had to contend. Goethe's *ad hominem* approach — and it is enlightening to insist on distinguishing such an approach from *ad personam* arguments, aimed at disqualifying a man on personal grounds — was dictated by the simple fact that such basic errors as reification are psychological in nature: 'Newton's character we would classify among the *rigid* types, just as his Theory of Colours is to be regarded as a *rigidified* aperçu' (HA, XIV, 173; my italics). Newton's cardinal error — an obsessive fixation with abstractions to the point where he deceives himself into taking them for realities — is born of the rigidity of the man who committed it — and *can* only be explained by recourse to character-analysis.

The intellectual virtues Goethe evinced in his scientific work — the modesty to recognize the limitations of his consciously amateur pursuits, coupled with the courage to insist on the reality of the insights he thereby gained — are also manifest in all the other areas of his many-sided activity. In the plastic arts, for example. After coming slowly to the painful conclusion that he simply lacked what it takes to be a painter, namely an 'Organ' to transform perception into the medium of paint and canvas, he studied and practised long and hard to become an amateur-connoisseur: one who could appreciate the great achievements of those endowed with a gift he himself did not possess. Indeed, it is not so much the *breadth* of Goethe's interests that strikes anyone reading his work on science, art, aesthetics, politics, or theatrical management — such wide-ranging interests are, to judge from the pages of the *Radio Times,* quite commonplace. What is astonishing is the passionate concentration yielding the hard-won *depth* of his knowledge — so different from the rather tepid 'coverage' that the media, inhibited by the Expert, too often deem fit for the layman's consumption. Nor is there anything of the *poseur* about Goethe's many-sidedness. He did not go out of his way to cultivate the image of a polymath; he speaks of the things that interested him as 'Gegenstände, die in meinem Wege lagen' (Eckermann, 1 February 1827). Just as his interest in geology was, in part, stimulated by his duties as minister responsible for the mines in his tiny duchy, so his biological studies were, he tells us ('Geschichte meiner botanischen Studien'; HA, XIII, 153-4), the result of a whole complex of factors, ranging from the spate of great scientific advances in the last quarter of the eighteenth century to the personal charm of a young enthusiast. Moreover, each and every one of his multiple side-lines was directly and indirectly related to his own central specialization, that of a poet. In that disarmingly frank 'Selbstschilderung' of 1797 where he proudly confesses his amateurism in science and painting, he draws the reader's attention to his 'poetic formative drive':

> The nodal point and the basis of his existence is a poetic formative drive, continuously and ever more deeply at work, both within and without; once one has grasped it, all other, seeming contradictions resolve themselves.

The practice of poetry and life-long reflection on its principles gave him an insight into form and formation that stood him in good stead in his other activities. And, reciprocally, his scientific and other interests provided him not only with material, with *Stoff*, for his poetic productions: 'da doch selbst dem Dichter, den die

Natur entschieden dazu bestimmt haben mag, erst Leben und Wissenschaft den Stoff geben, ohne welchen seine Arbeiten immer leer bleiben müssten' (letter to J.J. Erickson of 28 April 1797). They also, quite literally, 'in-formed' his poetic practice with a heightened awareness of living form. It is by virtue of this essential integration that Goethe can meaningfully speak of his activities as 'symbolic' (Eckermann, 2 May 1824): all of his interests embody a fundamental drive to perceive and make living, significant, forms. Such unity also entitles us to speak of him, if not as a Universal Man, equally proficient in a multiplicity of fields, then as a Whole Man — a man of parts, as Wilkinson and Willoughby have convincingly argued[2] — whose varied but interrelated activities are grounded in one central impulse.

In his writings on science, as in those on art and other matters, Goethe has left a body of work that is clearly designed to serve as a stimulant, whatever our gifts and whatever our limitations. He offers a paradigm, an *eminenter Fall,* of a human life intelligently lived. Not that he ever dreamt that much good would come from copying him, from trying to repeat his particular life-pattern. He had rather, like any born educator, an unshakable faith in his fellow men's interest in what interested him — in what Sir Karl Popper has called 'the problem of cosmology': 'the problem of understanding the world, including ourselves, and our knowledge, as part of the world'.[3] This incurable didacticism — which went hand in hand with his indefatigable amateurism — was further reinforced by his belief that *everyone* is capable of using his God-given apparatus to respond sensitively and intelligently to his environment:

> Experiencing, looking, observing, contemplating, connecting, discovering, inventing are mental activities which, singly and severally, are exercised a thousand-fold by more or less gifted people . . . . From these various powers named here, and many other related ones, Mother Nature has excluded no-one. (WA, ii, XI, 65)

If he grew impatient with the Arts Faculties of his day, and did all he could to encourage the newly-founded Science Faculties, it was not out of any wilful, Mephistophelian negation by a professional of an area of specialization he found unduly restrictive. He hoped rather that the disciplined investigation of nature would quicken in others, as it had in him, the defining quality of the true *amateur* — that sensitive discernment of significant form, wherever it be found, that alone shapes our inner life, and thus fosters our humanity. Perhaps I might conclude with a passage from Goethe's letter to Knebel of 25 November 1808 that the editor of this volume has often quoted, in and out of lectures. I offer it here in her deliberately provocative rendering:

> For more than a century now the humanities have ceased to humanize those who practise them. And it is a real blessing that Nature has stepped in, attracted attention to herself, and thus opened up the way to humanity from that angle.

It is an aspiration that both illuminates and endorses the whole complex, co-operative, enterprise of modern education.

Notes to Last Universal Man — or Wilful Amateur?

1. References wherever possible are to the Hamburger Ausgabe (abbreviated as HA);otherwise to the Weimarer Ausgabe (abbreviated as WA). Short essays are referred to by title only.

2. Elizabeth M. Wilkinson, 'The Poet as Thinker', in *German Studies Presented to L.A. Willoughby* (Oxford, 1952); and L.A. Willoughby, 'Unity and Continuity in Goethe', The Taylorian Lecture, 1946. Both reprinted in *Goethe. Poet and Thinker,* pp. 133-52 and 214-28. See, too, their article '"The Whole Man", in Schiller's Theory of Culture and Society: On the Virtue of a Plurality of Models' in *Essays in German Language, Culture and Society*, edited by Siegbert S. Prawer, R. Hinton Thomas and Leonard Forster (London, 1969), pp. 177-210.

3. *The Logic of Scientific Discovery* (London, 1959), p. 15.

Goethe and the Lied Hans Keller

'To make them' — Goethe's poems, that is — 'even more intelligible to the mind and the heart', our Chairman just said. And I'm spontaneously adopting his phrase as the motto of my lecture because, although he himself may not have been aware of the fact, it is capable of an entirely ambiguous interpretation. It is indeed all-important for us to clear our minds about the question of *how* great music makes poetry 'even more intelligible to the mind and the heart', if it ever does so at all. Before I plunge right into the heart of this matter, however, let me remind you, Ladies and Gentlemen, that 1982 rolls three years into one: the Stravinsky year, the Haydn year and the Goethe year. Accordingly we have already had a flood of words about each of these three geniuses — a flood of words but a dearth of facts and thoughts. In the case of Stravinsky, it is of course far too early to come to a conclusion about the character of his genius, although I have tried to do so in a recently published book.[1] In the case of Haydn, the public has been gravely misled, in that everybody talks about a Haydn renaissance right across our musical world; in my submission, Haydn's first birth has not yet taken place. What I mean is this: the great string quartets of Haydn, of which there are no fewer than forty-five, ought to assume the same position in the lives of both string-quartet players and their listeners as does Bach's *Well-tempered Clavier* in the lives of pianists and *their* listeners. So long as that hasn't happened, Haydn has not yet been born; the crucial facts about Haydn are not yet known.

Now, why do I devote the climax of my first paragraph to the

circumstance that the crucial thoughts and facts about Haydn are
not yet known? Because I think that in the case of Goethe,
likewise, there is at least one crucial fact which until now has either
been concealed or hasn't been realized at all. We've already had
that aforementioned flood of words about him; though, admittedly,
there have been exceptions — such as the talk on Radio 3 by the
editor of this volume, for example, which I found outstandingly
factual and outstandingly thoughtful.[2] But there has, of course,
also been the opposite: to wit, sheer gas — as in another Radio 3
talk, i.e. Thomas Mann's on 8 April. I don't know how many of
you heard it: it was a repeat of his 1949 broadcast. Suffice it to say
that I've never heard so much nonsense compressed into so short
a time. If you can explain to me why he should have juxtaposed
Luther, Bismarck and Goethe, you will merely have been able to
adduce his motives, as distinct from any reasons. And when,
climactically, he drew attention to the fact that Luther was
'profoundly musical', he evidently meant to imply that here was a
factor which linked Luther with Goethe. At this point I would
have turned off if I'd been alone in the room. For as far as music is
concerned, the only thing one can say about Goethe in this
context is that he was genuinely, profoundly *un*musical; and it is
this fact which, to my knowledge, hasn't yet been demonstrated. I
choose my words advisedly: I do mean *demonstrated*; for it isn't
very difficult to demonstrate Goethe's unmusicality. Those of you
who know his complete works will no doubt be aware of a draft he
composed — together with Schiller — in 1799, at the age of fifty: a
draft of an essay on dilettantism and on what the dilettante ought
and ought not to do. It has, I believe, not been translated. In it he
drew attention to — amongst other things — the advantages and
disadvantages of the art of music for the dilettante: to its
usefulness, its *Nutzen*, on the one hand; to the harm, the *Schaden*, it
might do him, on the other. Now at this point please listen
carefully, because you won't believe what you hear if you don't!
The advantages are said to be (a) that music is a useful pastime
(yes, a *Zeitvertreib*) and (b) that it educates the aural sense. Apart
from that there is the occasional advantage of what Goethe calls
'mechanical application', i.e. the subject's physical application to
an instrument — which is the only other advantage he is capable
of listing. The harm which music may do, on the other hand, is
great; because music leads to thoughtlessness — Goethe's word is

Gedankenleerheit — and to sensuality — *Sinnlichkeit*. Aside from these observations, the only thing Goethe has to add about the art of music is that it is a subjective art springing from the pleasure-drive (the *Lusttrieb*), which he seems to conceive in the approximate sense of Freud's pleasure principle, the *Lustprinzip*. Well now, anyone who is capable of putting on paper what I have now reported, in fact largely quoted to you, cannot possibly be regarded as musical. When Felix Mendelssohn came to visit Goethe and tried his unsuccessful best to explain music to him, he ought to have told him what, alas, he only wrote to a friend of his.[3] And that was that music couldn't be conveyed in words, not because it was too *vague*, but because it was too well-defined; far better defined than words, far too 'definite' (*bestimmt*). In that same note Mendelssohn added that musical thought is the only kind of human thought which says the same thing to different people as long as they are musical enough to understand it. Whereas words, and their underlying conceptual thought, don't say the same thing to different people.

That Mendelssohn is absolutely right can be proved; as long as we rid ourselves of the prejudice that music is an abstract art. On the contrary, musical thought is the concretest mode of thought of which the human mind is capable: far more concrete, that is to say, than conceptual thought. Let us think of a concrete conceptual term such as 'table': when we say 'table' our addressee is still free to imagine a million different tables in his own mind. We haven't, although we have used the concretest of terms, told him anything concrete about what we are talking about. Whereas when we utter a meaningful musical thought — I repeat, a *meaningful* musical thought — it only means itself; so that there is no degree of abstraction whatsoever. There will, of course, be abstraction in proportion as it gets less meaningful: a musical cliché is a well-known abstraction used by many who are not capable of conceiving meaningful new musical thoughts. Meaningful new musical thoughts, however, are invariably, inevitably, ineluctably, unavoidably concrete to an extreme degree: there simply is no abstraction involved in the formulation of a meaningful musical thought. It is quite obvious, then, that Goethe was incapable of musical thought as such; for had he been capable of it, he would have come to a conclusion which would at least have been comparable to what Mendelssohn said about music. And significantly enough, Goethe wasn't happy when Mendelssohn played to him, or rather when he *only* played to him: the composer had to *talk* to him about the music he played. In other words, Mendelssohn had to do the very thing which he said you could not do: explain in 'indefinite' words what the 'definite' music meant.

This introduction, Ladies and Gentlemen, was absolutely necessary for the purpose of elucidating (a) the relation of Goethe to the lied and (b) the question of how far great music, great songs are capable of conveying deeper knowledge about the poems of which they are the settings. As far as the relation of Goethe to the lied is concerned, the answer, though not simple, can be compressed with crystal clarity into a single sentence: the great lied does to Goethe what Goethe did to the lied. Let me now explain what this sentence means, since I see plenty of half-raised eyebrows amongst you. Owing, I suppose, to the fact that you don't understand what I'm talking about when I say that Goethe 'did' something to the lied, when in reality he was passionately in favour, not of pure poetry, but of what is described as 'poesia per musica', i.e. of poetry which avails itself of the help of music. So unmusically fond was he of this musical approach to poetry that a vast number of his own poems were written against the background of pre-existent melodies, be they folk tunes, chiefly German folk-songs (all of which are lousy), Lutheran chorales, or even Italian and English compositions. He loved writing his poems into existing songs, in the hope that, inasmuch as he thus seemed to satisfy musical requirements, it would be all the easier for future or contemporary composers to re-compose those poems to music. You will perhaps understand a little better now what I mean when I say that great music, the great lied, does to Goethe what Goethe did to the lied. Because what Goethe did to the lied — the method was called 'parody' and the products were called *contrafacta*, i.e. counterfeits — was that, regardless of what a particular lied had expressed, regardless of the words it had set to music, *he* quite often wrote strongly contrasting words into the self-same song and thus used it merely as a means: as metric material, for the purpose of conveying his own poetry.

In other, and perhaps preciser words, he used those songs as formal background: as *form* against whose background he threw his own individual *structures* into relief. You note that I call 'form' that which plenty of works, plenty of pieces, have in common; whereas 'structure' I reserve for that which is characteristic of a single work, a single piece. Goethe used the form of those songs he availed himself of — primarily of course their metre, and metre is a stable element of form — for the purpose of defining his own individual poetic rhythms against their metric background. Just as the great composers used Goethe's poems, that is the form of Goethe's poems, their metre, as background, as mere material, as a means of throwing their own individual musical structures into relief, and thus defining them. All the great composers did, then, was to take music's revenge as it were: what Goethe had done to music by changing those songs in order to make them fit *his* poems, they did to Goethe in that they used his poems for the purpose of creating rhythmic tensions between *their* musical foreground and the poetic background, thus expressing genuinely musical meaning. (And, mind you, Goethe did not believe in the expressive nature of music which he did not think was an expressive art).

The musical meanings of the great lied composers, then — of many of them at any rate — could not have been expressed without that particular background: without the background of Goethe's poems. In other and shorter words: what the great composers did was to use the verbal metre of Goethe's poems, together with the conceptual meaning of the words, as something which was 'fore-hearable', predictable, and could thus be meaningfully contradicted by the music. A tension could then be established between the rhythm of the music and the metre of the words. That is to say: the verbal metre, forehearable, concretely expectable as it was, formed a stable background against which the music's rhythm, its tensions as against the metre, could be meaningfully expressed. And by such meaningful contradiction I mean one which does not merely contradict what is expected, but which at the same time establishes a relation with what one expects; and what one expects in the case of poems always happens anyhow, just because one *does* hear the words of the poem. To that extent, the verbal rhythm and the verbal metre are retained. At the same time, however, we hear the music's rhythm, and hear the tensions which are established between the verbal rhythm and metre on the one hand and the music's rhythm on the other.

Small wonder, then, that Goethe disliked virtually all the great songs that were written to his poetry. Whereas he liked a great number of *small* songs — songs which don't contradict his verbal rhythm and metre: they simply form a useful bit of background noise and leave the verbal metre, and indeed the conceptual meaning, of the poem perfectly intact. That kind of song he liked; but we have first-hand evidence that Goethe strongly disliked some of the greatest settings of Schubert and Beethoven. And rightly so, from his own, from the poetic point of view: a great poem is a great poem is a great poem — and that's it. A masterpiece is perfect: you can't do anything about it. Accepting its wholeness, you can't set it to music, unless the music is musically meaningless — a purely sensuous background noise which leaves the poem untouched. Yes, that is easily possible. But you can't do something equally inspired about that perfect masterpiece and yet hope to leave it intact. Once you're a great composer, and therefore inevitably use that poem as metric material for your own musical purposes, you will harm the purely conceptual meaning of the poem: something new will be engendered. And here I come back to our opening question, a question I promised you the answer to: and that is the extent to which the great composer tells our minds and hearts even more about what the poem is talking about than the poem itself does.

Well, it all depends on what we mean by 'even more'. If we mean by it something which could have been expressed in words, then the answer is 'No'. Through words — and I am thinking only of Goethe's poetic masterpieces — Goethe expressed as much about the subject in question as was conceivably expressible. If, on the other hand, we mean something which can *not* be conveyed through words; something which is only musically expressible, or at least best expressible, in music; something which, in words, would be far vaguer, and could only be 'definitely' expressed in music (as Mendelssohn reminds us), then our Chairman's observation was absolutely right. In that respect and to that extent (which is a very wide extent), it is indeed possible for the great composer to contribute something about the state of psychological affairs behind a great poem which the poem itself could not have expressed, could only have alluded to.

Now then: Am I right or am I wrong? If I'm right, it follows that different settings of the same poem will be very different. You will say that may also be the case if I'm wrong; because it is entirely possible — and I'm now interpreting what you look as though you're thinking — for one great composer to express *part* of the meaning of a poem, and for another great composer to express a complementary part of that poem's meaning. We would then be confronted with two or more different songs which, nevertheless, would express no more than the poet himself had intended to express: each composer would then have expressed a part of the truth. Granted that those different songs might indeed be different even if I'm wrong, as soon as they *contradict* each other I'm bound to be right! As soon as it can be shown — and of course I'm now talking in terms of intra-musical meaning — that, purely musically, one setting of the poem straightforwardly contradicts another, both of them being equally loved, both of them being equally embraced by everybody (except of course Goethe himself), then you will have to accept that I'm right. In order to give you this practical demonstration I have selected two Goethe poems and three settings of each of the two.

I'm starting with the poem 'Meeresstille' of which I have selected three settings, the second and third of which you will know already: Schubert's and Beethoven's, both of them written, interestingly enough, in the same year — 1815. But the first is by someone whose name you may not even know — Charles Tomlinson Griffes. And the only reason I picked him is that had Goethe known this American composer who studied — and even taught — in Berlin, he would have been the one whose setting our poet really would have loved! Simply because it doesn't add a thing: it goes parallel with the verbal metre, makes the appropriate noises, in the right places, about what the poem is concretely describing — and is a bore from first note to last. I promise you that if this composer (who was unfortunately born in 1884 and died in 1920) had lived in Goethe's own time, he would, in Goethe's opinion, have been *the* outstanding Goethe-composer. And for much the same sort of reason as Goethe suggested when — juxtaposing Karl Friedrich Zelter's 'Erlking' and Schubert's 'Erlking' — he judged Zelter's setting a supreme achievement and Schubert's, quite rightly, as something which harmed his poem. As indeed it does! For, as I have explained, it is inevitable that you harm your material if that material is itself a masterpiece. You have to *use* it; whereas a masterpiece has to be left untouched: as

soon as you touch it, you harm it. What I am saying, then, is that
Charles Tomlinson Griffes leaves 'Meeresstille' boringly untouched.[4] Hence Goethe would have been delighted: the music is
utterly meaningless; it is best described as a successful student's
exercise — successful in that it meets all the melodic and
harmonic requirements one would impose upon a student.
Artistically, however, it is proportionately *un*successful, in that it
does not contradict any of the expectations it arouses; on the
contrary, it meets expectation after expectation, having just
aroused them by way of both its own musical premises and the
regular metre of the poem itself — which, almost grotesquely, is
strictly followed. Not the slightest tension is established between
the music's rhythm and the poem's metre; in fact, strictly
speaking, the music's rhythm doesn't exist. There is the music's
metre which is identical with the poem's metre, and that is all
there is to it.

As soon as we move on to the Schubert setting, by contrast, we
notice the very deliberate friction he established between the
music's harmonic rhythm and the metre of both the music and
the poem — especially at the line 'Keine Luft von keiner Seite,
Todesstille fürchterlich'; or 'In der ungeheuern Weite reget keine
Welle sich'.

I don't want to go into technical detail: this is not a musicological
lecture. But I am quite sure that my pointers are sufficiently
concrete for you to be alive to what I am talking about. I merely
have to add that Schubert characteristically succeeds in com-
pressing his setting into a matter of thirty-two bars. It's almost a
musical aphorism, into which he injects an unbelievable amount
of contrasting musical meanings. For the rest, what a violent
contradiction of the setting by Charles Tomlinson Griffes! Now
we see what a great composer does to, and about, a great poem.

But it is when we come to Beethoven's setting that we get the
most drastic contradictions of both musical as well as verbal
metrical expectations; the fiercest contradictions conceivable,
over-obvious to the naked ear. In fact, far from composing it as an
aphorism, Beethoven turns the song into an extended structure:
the Schubert song comprises thirty-two bars; whereas the
Beethoven setting comprises seventy-three bars of the same type
— more than twice Schubert's duration. If you are conscious of
the enormous, contrasting roles which 'steps' and 'leaps' —

'conjunct motion' and 'disjunct motion' — can play in music, you will immediately understand that Beethoven uses Goethe's poem as mere emotional, tonal and, of course, metric material; remaining still entirely respectful towards its conceptual meaning, but at the same time being absolutely intent upon expressing, communicating, conveying thoughts which can only be expressed musically, and which, to that extent, have nothing to do with Goethe's own meaning, although they are closely linked with it emotionally. May I once again draw your attention to 'Keine Luft von keiner Seite, Todesstille fürchterlich' and 'In der ungeheuern Weite reget keine Welle sich'. Beethoven's 'Weite' wholly contradicts Schubert's: in itself it isn't even a step, — the second syllable continues the vastly sustained note of the first; but the octave leap to 'reget' completes a complex piece of multi-dimensional musical philosophy. Horizontally (i.e. melodically) expressed, we get the feeling of both horizontal 'width' (*Weite*) — the 'wide', i.e. sustained note and its repetition — and vertical 'width': the ensuing octave leap. By now any conceptual aspect of physical width, distance, endlessness has been forgotten.

Beethoven is not even prepared to let Goethe's poem stand as it is. No; for purely musical purposes, he repeats the opening lines at the end — something which would make a shocking effect if we were reading the poem without the music, but which is the only possible solution once we hear and understand Beethoven's major structure. The more so since he composed this Goethe poem together with another one, 'Glückliche Fahrt', calling the entire work 'Meeresstille und Glückliche Fahrt' ('Calm Sea and Prosperous Voyage'). The enlarged structure demands an extended texture: Beethoven scored his Op. 112 for soprano, alto, tenor, bass, and orchestra.

I think we are now in a position to complete our answer to the opening question our Chairman inspired. What the greatest music tells us about the subject of a great poem is an entirely new communication about a psychological complex: I have to use these wholly abstract words for what, in musical reality, is absolutely concrete. And I am talking about a complex of both conscious and unconscious feelings, not an exclusively unconscious 'complex' in the Freudian sense. We recognize it as having been latently, potentially, in us before we heard the music. But now, for the first time, we have encountered and experienced a well-defined proof of its existence, a formulation that is felt to be, not 'about' it, but simply *it*. 'That's it' is, therefore, the highest praise we can extend to a piece of meaningful music. Goethe's own beloved concept of 'poesia per musica' does not really make sense in the case of great music. For where great music is concerned, only the opposite relation — to wit 'musica per poesia' — can meaningfully obtain, in that the music in question uses poetry for the purpose of expressing its own independent meaning. And by 'independent' I mean that which cannot be formulated through any means other than musical.

My next song will make this little theory of musical cognition even clearer. It is 'Wanderers Nachtlied'; and I am referring you to the settings of Loewe, Wolf, and Schubert. This time, at least, you won't have to concern yourself with any rubbish! For even the Loewe song, the weakest of the three, does establish a minimum of rhythmic tension which turns the music into something that contributes meaning unavailable in the poem itself.

It is at the line 'Süsser Friede, komm', ach komm' in meine Brust!' that the three composers contradict each other most lavishly; and quite especially Wolf and Schubert. Wolf, in fact, explicitly requires you to sing that particular passage 'sehr weich und ausdrucksvoll' (very tenderly and expressively); whereas Schubert simply writes 'etwas geschwinder' (a little faster) — which, in effect, is the precise opposite. Yet both of them make extreme musical sense, little as Goethe would have liked their respective senses. And while Loewe's setting is twenty bars long, the Wolf song, which is a very substantial piece, is thirty-two bars, and presents us with an additional complication which Goethe — and indeed any composer at Goethe's time — would have found quite intolerable, in that it starts in one key (G flat major) and ends in another (B major!). That is to say, it is written in so-miscalled 'progressive tonality'; and through such a dramatic key procedure it changes the course of psychological events far more drastically than does either of the other two songs. For this purpose, Wolf does indeed need a more extended structure; hence the thirty-two bars.

From Schubert, on the other hand, we get one of the highest peaks of compression in the entire history of composition. He deals with the poem in a mere eleven bars and, at the same time, expresses a wealth of contrasting, yet continually consistent, emotions such as no other composer — with the possible exception of two — has ever conveyed within a comparable space. One of my two exceptions you will be able to guess: it is Chopin. But the other who succeeded on at least one or two occasions deserves, as pre-eminently a song composer, the closest possible comparison: it is — don't shoot me — George Gershwin.

The end is in sight, Ladies and Gentlemen; there are three more minutes to suffer. In his book *Style and Idea* Schoenberg confesses that he had grown into quite a mature man and composer, who knew his Schubert songs virtually by heart, when he suddenly realized that he had never bothered about the texts: that he had, in fact, no idea what those texts were, whose they were, or what they conveyed. With a more than uneasy conscience, then, he rushed to his scores in order to read up, chiefly the Goethe poems, but also some others — only to find that he hadn't missed anything at all. Not that he is implying that he thought those Goethe poems weren't any good. Not at all! What he *does* mean is that for the purpose of getting the full meaning of 'musica per poesia' there was no need to understand the *poesia*, because the musical meaning made itself felt with crystal clarity against what I call the background of both the metre of the poem *and* indeed the conceptual meaning of the words — as one heard them while listening to the music. Far be it from either Schoenberg or myself to suggest that a great song makes a great poem unimportant; but for the duration of the experience of the song the experience of the original, the extra-musical meaning of the poem is not of essential significance. It will, of course, help to know what the poem is 'about'. It will help doubly if one has had a real artistic experience of the poem — but only if one is prepared to tolerate its 'destruction' for the duration of the musical experience. That destruction is only temporary; for after the music is all over the poem resumes its rightful place. But as long as we listen to the poem with verbal, conceptual veneration while the music is going on, we are behaving in a passive way. In much the same way as that first Goethe composer I discussed tonight behaved when he harmlessly set 'Meeresstille' to music, his creative passivity replacing the creative act — a busily active passivity, to be sure. In order to do great music justice we have, by contrast, to take part, for the length of its duration, in the active destruction of the great poem it both does and does not serve.

Notes to Goethe and the Lied

1. Hans Keller and Milein Cosman, *Stravinsky Seen and Heard* (London, Toccata Press, 1982).

2. Published here, for the first time, on pp. 171ff. below.

3. Letter to Marc André Souchay of 15 October 1842.

4. A gramophone recording is available: New World Records, NW 273, stereo.

Covert Confessions: The Tension between Goethe and Schiller, a Prelude to Modernism Karl Heinz Bohrer

The Challenge thrown down

A few days before his forty-fifth birthday Goethe received a letter which was to lead to a ten-year-long correspondence. A letter which thirty years later he himself would not hesitate to claim as 'a great gift proffered to the German people, I might even say to mankind itself' (to Zelter, 30 October 1824). It was Schiller's well-known letter of 23 August 1794. A letter quite exceptional in the epistolary literature known to me, being pregnant with consequences, not only for the two men themselves, but for the whole history of Goethe's subsequent 'image', including his elevation to a figure of sacral proportions. What Schiller was after all undertaking here, and in a way as psychologically hazardous as it was philosophically significant, was to lead someone he as yet scarcely knew towards a theoretical understanding of *himself as artist* — while at the same time glossing, in terms both reflective and dramatic, that famous antithesis between 'experience' and 'idea' which had been the focus of a conversation between them a few months earlier on the subject of Goethe's 'Urpflanze'. Goethe's own interpretation of the 'enormous gulf' he had always — until that crucial conversation — sensed between their two modes of thinking is recorded much later in an autobiographical piece entitled 'Propitious Happening' of 1817 (HA, X, 538f.). And this did much to foster the long-prevailing *typological* interpretation of the difference between them while contributing little to its *historical* understanding. According to this latter account Schiller had reacted to Goethe's visual representation of a 'symbolic plant' with the now famous remark: 'That's no experience! That's an *idea*!' To which Goethe had retorted: 'How nice to learn that I have ideas without knowing it! And actually *see* them with my own eyes too' (HA, X, 540f.).

What Schiller's letter in fact does is to present Goethe with a challenging attempt at interpreting such professed innocence of 'ideas' coupled with an almost coquettishly conceded addiction to sense-perception. And he does this, not just by recourse to psycho-typological explanations, but by reference to an axiom derived from the philosophy of history. According to this, the mark of the modern artist is that he is no longer conditioned by nature, but by history; no longer by space, but by time; no longer by eternity, but by epoch; no longer by perception, but by reflection. And for these related reasons he can no longer apprehend 'Nature' directly; he can only take hold of phenomena, which *seem* to be immediately presented to perception, through the medium of thought. Almost as if Schiller had feared that any such historico-theoretical explanation of the modern poet was bound to miss the essence of Goethe's own personal and artistic substance, his letter now endeavours — in sheet after freshly started sheet — to reconcile the phenomenon of Goethe's nature, so blissfully blessed by the spirit of antiquity, with his own, so painfully endured, spirit of modern intellectuality. And, to start with, Goethe's own 'method' is itself presented as a phenomenon:

> That observer's eye of yours, which lets its gaze rest with undistorting tranquillity on the phenomena to be observed, never exposes you to the danger of deviating on to paths along which philosophical speculation, no less than an arbitrary imagination obedient only to its own laws, may all too easily stray. In your unerring intuitive perception everything is already encompassed which analysis so laboriously has to seek. And far more completely! And it is only because it resides within you as indivisible whole that the richness you possess is concealed from yourself.

There follows an uncovering of the inherently problematic nature of this quality which Schiller sees as the essence of Goethe's genius. It is a passage in which agitation of feeling and nobility of spirit are contained by the language of sublimest drama. For the thirty-five-year-old Schiller now strips away whatever doubts and resentments he had hitherto entertained, and offers in their stead a moving act of homage in the grand style:

> For a long time now I have been following, albeit from a distance — but with constantly renewed wonder and admiration — the course on which your mind is set, and the path you have marked out for yourself. You seek the essential and necessary laws of nature. But you take the hardest way to pursue them: a way which any less sound and sturdy mind would do well to avoid.

The hardest way . . . ! As Schiller means it, this implies Goethe's unswerving devotion to natural phenomena still conceived as indivisible wholes. An 'heroic idea', he calls it. Because such a pursuit makes impossible demands on the potentialities of the modern poet, and postulates the unquestioning confidence of the men of antiquity:

> However — since you were born a German; since your Greek spirit was to find its incarnation in this Northern mode — you had no choice but *either* to become a Northern artist yourself, *or* to supply your imagination with those powers of which the accidents of time and place had deprived it. In other words: by taking thought, to bring to birth, as it were from within and by rational means, a land of Greece in our Northern clime.

With this interpretation of Goethe as a 'Modern Greek' Schiller has of course denied his claims to any immediate and unmediated experience of nature, and thereby implicitly anticipated the thesis he was soon to develop in his treatise *On Naive and Sentimental Poetry*, defending it systematically by means of categories borrowed from Kant: the modern artist, in order to resolve any conflict between the 'logical' and the 'aesthetic' has, in other words, no alternative but 'to transpose concepts back into intuition'. In so doing, however, Schiller was simply projecting problems of his own mode of creativity on to the objective situation of a Goethe: rather as if the latter produced unconsciously, i.e. 'naively', what he himself produced consciously, i.e. 'sentimentally'. Or to formulate it in terms of Peter Szondi's thesis: the 'Naive' becomes identical with the 'Sentimental'.[1]

The paradox of recognizing Goethe as a 'naive' type on the one hand — because of his unconscious dedication to phenomena as they are, his continuing obsession with 'things' — while, on the other hand, manifesting a sheer inability to accept this as anything other than the result of reflective processes: this is a paradox which may be veiled in Schiller's birthday tribute itself, and in letters immediately following it, but is never really resolved. Thus for all his avowed admiration Schiller is still, and even in this act of homage, denigrating Nature in favour of Reflection, by terming it 'mere' nature, exactly as he had done a year earlier — and to Goethe's not inconsiderable displeasure — in his essay *On Grace and Dignity*. But despite this Goethe's immediate response was unusually warm and appreciative. Indeed it comes close to a programmatic declaration of his own hope that they might henceforth, not simply 'join forces', but maybe subject the theme propounded by Schiller — the relation between conscious and unconscious in the creative process — to closer inspection by more precise reference to their different methods of working. Thus, in respect of his own case, he warns his venturesome new friend — without more ado and with open-hearted generosity — of things he may well be faced with on closer acquaintance:

> a kind of obscure tentativeness, a groping irresolution, of which I have never been able to become master even though I am only too aware of it. Yet such and kindred phenomena are common enough in our nature. And it is after all by our own nature that we are for the most part ready to be ruled — as long as it doesn't become too much of a tyrant.   (27 August 1794)

This last sentence indicates all the same that Goethe has no intention of taking leave of *his* own nature, or of any of the inherent 'phenomena' he has hinted at. And this despite the sovereign grace with which he will from now on accept Schiller as interpreter, indeed 'prophet' of his own dreams (26 April and 22 June 1796). At the same time this could well imply that he is, from now on and henceforth, not prepared to talk about the processes or products of his own creativity except in terms tentative, ironic, and oblique. And so we are faced with questions recurrently posed by scholars. Were Goethe and Schiller, apart from the joint programme of cultural propaganda they undertook in the service of a classicizing art, ever really at one?[2] How far did Goethe, who without any doubt gradually gained insight into the conceptual schemas Schiller had borrowed from Kant (even to the point of adopting the term 'sentimental' in his crucial letter of 16 August 1797) ever really grasp, let alone prove willing to assimilate, the arguments Schiller had derived from contemporary philosophy of history — and used to propound an entirely new theory of modernism in art and poetry? To what extent did Schiller's new formulation of the issues at stake in the old 'Querelle des anciens et des modernes'[3] — the question, namely, of the authority of antique models for modern poets — ever really present itself to Goethe as a problem in the dimension of historical time, and not just a problem of aesthetic immanence?

If Schiller's reckless, not to say tactless, challenge to Goethe seemed at first to have succeeded, then only because Goethe could recognize himself in the mirror it held up to him: in the metaphor, myth — or model — of a tension between North and South. The more so since Schiller had acclaimed his *Iphigenie* as a tragedy which could rank with those of the Greeks. The seventh of his *Roman Elegies*, nostalgic precipitate of his Italian Journey — the most significant event of his life before his encounter with Schiller — begins with the words:

> O wie fühl' ich in Rom mich so froh! gedenk ich der
> Zeiten,
> Da mich ein graulicher Tag hinten im Norden umfing,
> Trübe der Himmel und schwer auf meine Scheitel sich
> senkte,
> Farb- und gestaltlos die Welt um den Ermatteten lag,
> Und ich über mein Ich, des unbefriedigten Geistes
> Düstre Wege zu spähn, still in Betrachtung versank.

Such 'chimerical notions', as Goethe had also called them, now seemed to have been conceptually focussed by Schiller's formulation of the problematic nature of the Northern artist: his ever-questioning, never-satisfied spirit which, confronted by lack of form and colour, falls back upon itself and reflects about its Self. But now comes the essential difference! What to Schiller seemed a necessary condition of the process of artistic creation was to Goethe not really an act of mind at all, but a melancholic verging on hypochondria, in face of climatic and other geographic deficiencies, which could easily be remedied by travelling South! Such deficiencies, suffered in his very flesh, are not at all conceived as a condition of the modern artist; they are not thought of in the dimension of *time* at all, but disappear as soon as he experiences the reality, the presence of Rome. The mere change of place and objects — 'Gegenstände' — enables Goethe to make that leap across time and times which Schiller thought he had, by means of his own theory, put beyond the bounds of possibility.

> Stürze dich eilig ins Meer, um Morgen früher zu sehen,
> Was Jahrhunderte schon göttliche Lust dir gewährt . . .

we read in the fifteenth of his *Roman Elegies*. And it is his experience of the sheer physical presence of the sea and the soil of antiquity, with all their attendant mythology, which made him feel such a 'stranger' when he returned home in 1788 to find a Germany whose cultural temper was far more intellectualized. So that for all Schiller's own yearnings for Greece, for all their prompt recognition of a joint programme of literary propaganda, a gulf yawned which was not so easily to be bridged. Schiller had after all taken as his point of departure in that birthday letter an *idea*: the idea that a lack, a deficiency, was the very condition of the modern poet. Whereas Goethe out of his inmost nature, and from his very beginnings, had *felt* the exact opposite; had from the start hymned his own sense of the fulness of life as a privilege bestowed upon him by the gods. As in those famous lines he sent to his friend Gustgen Stolberg in 1777:

> Alles geben die Götter, die unendlichen,
> Ihren Lieblingen ganz,
> Alle Freuden, die unendlichen,
> Alle Schmerzen, die unendlichen, ganz.

What Schiller had done was to discover the dignity of the modern artist in his very deficiency: in his reflective powers, and his capacity for forming theories. Whereas Goethe, while still in Italy, expressly distanced himself from any such vindication of a 'Northern' type. On his avoidance of friends from home he wrote on 27 October 1787:

> For that my way of seeing things would not be theirs I
> know all the more clearly because of my efforts during
> this last year to rid myself of those chimerical notions and
> modes of thought typical of the North, and get used to
> breathing and seeing more freely under this vaulted
> blue. (HA, XI, 430)

Goethe simply enjoyed the physical reality of classical antiquity. It
presented him with no problems arising from historical remote-
ness. The history of Rome, history in general, may be quoted in
his letters and reports; but it is always understood as 'Nature'.
Whether it appears as 'history of the world' or as 'millenia' (HA, XI,
147, 346), history appears always, whether in the *Roman Elegies* or
the *Italian Journey*, in the sense of a natural phenomenon:

> When one contemplates such an 'existence', which is
> more than two thousand years old, so variously changed
> through changing times, fundamentally different and yet
> still the same — the same soil, the same land, the same
> hill, sometimes even the same walls and pillars, and in
> the people still traces of their ancient character — then
> one becomes a participator in the great counsels and
> decrees of Fate. It becomes difficult from the very start to
> imagine how Rome followed upon Rome; and not just
> the new upon the old, but the various epochs of old and
> new, one upon another. (HA, XI, 130f.)

Goethe, then, sees himself not as a contemporary of 'fate', its
'Zeit-genosse', but a 'Mit-genosse', a sharer in its joys. He's never
really trying to get in touch with *history*, but with what he called the
'tremendous' quality of those objects, those 'Gegen-stände' from
the past. With that about them which makes one 'tremble' and
thus engages our contemplation so intensely that we stand before
them in awe and wonder. This is a transposing of time into space.
And it is this that is the characteristic order of Goethe's imagination.

From Schiller's standpoint, however, such a way of experiencing
historical epochs was, quite literally, ana-chronistic: beyond time.
And the suspicion is not unfounded that Goethe's whole object-
relatedness was diametrically opposed to Schiller's attempt to
mediate between them, whether tentatively as in his birthday

letter or, later on, as full-blown theorem in *Naive and Sentimental Poetry*. For this theorem, when it appeared *in extenso*, was not concerned with a reconciliation between North and South at all; nor even with mediating between the art of the Ancients and the Moderns; but with the essentially reflective character of *all* modern art — regardless of whether the individual artist happens to be of the naive or of the sentimental type. Whereas Goethe, even after his return from Italy, remained — both theoretically and practically — outside this whole conceptual constellation as developed from Schiller, through Schlegel and Hölderlin, to Hegel. Coming from the explorations of Italian art and nature he had undertaken with Heinrich Meyer and Karl Philip Moritz he found himself subjectively overwhelmed, and objectively over-taxed, by Schiller's ruthless attempts to claim his allegiance for a theory he was intellectually unprepared for, and disinclined to respond to by any explicit theorizing of his own — preferring to fall back on such oblique intimations of the mystery of art as he would present in his enigmatic *Märchen* written for their journal *Die Horen*.[4] It has rightly been argued that such a sophisticated Kantian as Schiller could at this stage all too easily have humiliated his conceptually unpractised friend, both intellectually and morally, by demonstrating the inherently anachronistic nature of his position. And the temptation to do so must have been exacerbated, not only by Goethe's express indifference to arguments about the philosophy of history, but by his evident disregard of the intellectual temper of his own epoch in particular; a neglect which had left him, during the six years between his return from Italy and the start of his friendship with Schiller, isolated and lonely. It was after all an epoch marked by the French Revolution. Its reflection in the early Romantics' philosophy of history during the 'nineties — Friedrich Schlegel, Novalis, Fichte and the young Hegel — had repercussions far into the nineteenth century. The whole 'feel' of this epoch, indeed the very concept of 'epoch' itself, as an unmistakably new kind of energy such as had never been seen before — this was something Goethe was not able to go along with. Such arguments are in no way invalidated by a remark he made when he accompanied his Duke on their *Campagne in Frankreich*: 'In this place, at this time, an entirely new epoch in world-history is being born. And to be able to say "We were there"!' (HA, X, 235). For if one considers the way this war-correspondent (which is what Goethe in fact was) presented the failure of the Prusso-Austrian campaign against Revolutionary France, one cannot fail to be struck by his total absence of insight into the historical significance of political events. And one is forced to ask oneself wherein precisely in Goethe's eyes lay the epoch-making nature of the French Revolution. In an idea to which he had never given positive assent? Or merely in the factual thusness of a military failure or success which would have consequences in the game of *Machtpolitik*? It is typical of a certain abstemiousness vis-à-vis the philosophy of history, distinguishing him from his German contemporaries, that Goethe should have reserved the notion of 'epoch' for his purely private 'Annalen'. Thus in his thank-you letter for Schiller's 'challenge' he dates 24 August 1794 as the start of 'a new epoch'. And in a letter to his close friend, Zelter, thirty years later characterizes his correspondence with Schiller as 'testimony of an "epoch" now past, and which will not come again, yet whose effects are still at work right down to this very day'. But that of course was in the perspective of conciliatory retrospect. At the time the new epoch didn't look anything like so rosy! And among the *Xenien* published over their joint initials in Schiller's *Musenalmanach für das Jahr 1797* we may read in tones of phlegmatic misanthropy:

Der Zeitpunkt

Eine grosse Epoche hat das Jahrhundert geboren,
   Aber der grosse Moment findet ein kleines Geschlecht
                              (HA, I, 209)

It is, in short, doubtful whether Goethe ever understood 'der grosse Moment' except as a moment great with possibilities: 'a pregnant moment', freed of all temporal limitations, such as Lessing had postulated when discoursing on the classical sculptor's choice of subject in his *Laokoon*. It was after all precisely the 'momentariness' of events which had so disconcerted him in the French Revolution. And precisely because their chaotic nature destroyed the only acceptable form of 'momentariness' hitherto available to him: that which he had discovered for himself in Italy and after — the 'felt' reality of the enduring permanence of the present moment. This understanding is exemplified and illuminated by the way he records a single scene in his account of a Roman carnival. It is a description which anticipates our contemporary techniques of 'shock'. The celebrations ended with

> a sudden, violent, momentary 'impression', eagerly
> awaited and briefly enjoyed by thousands, of whom but a
> few would be able to say thereafter why they were so
> expectant, or why they had so relished the moment when
> it came.   (HA, XI, 507f.)

In this passage, where Goethe so clearly recognizes such
'momentary' effects in a way which is positively crying out for
more precise aesthetic analysis, he at the same time comes up
against the point which is fundamentally at odds with his own
classical *credo*. For 'the supreme, the vital enjoyment', he writes,
'derived precisely from the fact that its manifestation was purely
momentary'. This is a point which was not to be consciously, or at
least discursively, formulated until the avant-garde movement of
the late nineteenth century.

What Goethe was however disposed to applaud aesthetically, as
sheer momentary appearance, he promptly distances himself
from when it comes to moral judgment. As later, in *Elective
Affinities* or his *Novelle*, he disputes the value of all such 'momentary
manifestations' because they 'leave no trace at all behind in the
[structure or texture of the] psyche'. And as if to leave nothing
open to doubt in this respect he attaches purely negative
ideological connotations to moments of enjoyment so primitive
that they don't even qualify for ethical evaluation. They may be
manifestations of 'liberty' and 'equality'; but only of a kind that
can be enjoyed in a state of manic frenzy (HA, XI, 515). In a passage
of his essay on Winckelmann which may date back to the time
before he received Schiller's letter, and expresses the 'horror'
inspired in him by the events of the Terror, Goethe sketched a
view of the world which, oblivious of the contemporary sense of
time as epoch and history, sees man only in the dimension of
cosmic time and space:

> For what would be the point of all this expenditure of
> suns and moons and planets, of stars and galaxies and the
> milky way, of comets and nebula, of worlds evolved and
> still evolving — if at the end of it all a happy man cannot
> have spontaneous unreflecting joy of his own existence?
>   (HA, XII, 98; cf. 595ff.)

It is not surprising that such a distanced attitude to the revolutionary *Zeitgeist*, his turning away from it to natural history and philosophy, should have alienated Goethe, not only from former friends such as the politically committed Georg Forster, but from many who were far from being supporters of the French Revolution. He wrote about his sense of isolation in the section of his *Campagne in Frankreich* dated November 1792:

> My scientific studies didn't fare much better. The passion with which I pursued them seemed incomprehensible to everyone. No one could understand that it sprang from my innermost being; they took this praiseworthy endeavour for a wayward whim. As far as they were concerned I had better things to do with my talents, and should continue to give them free rein in poetry and the arts. They felt themselves all the more justified in this because my way of thinking didn't fit in with theirs. On the contrary: in most respects it was the very opposite. It's hard to imagine anyone more isolated than I was during those years, and remained for a long time to come.

Such, then, was the mental, spiritual, and psychological state of affairs that Schiller's challenge was to light on. Yet on Goethe's own admission that letter and those which followed worked like an *elixir vitae*, obviously touching on something that had hitherto remained hidden. More than this: if according to Schiller's aesthetic theory the criterion of Modernism was to be the self-reflecting and reflective work of art, then it was Goethe himself who, with his *Wilhelm Meister*, was to create the prototype of this new mode of art. So at any rate decreed Friedrich Schlegel, leader of the early Romantic movement, in his review of that novel at the turn of the century (No. 216 of his *Athenäum*). Entirely in the spirit of the new history of philosophy he offered it in the form of a now famous theorem: 'The French Revolution, Fichte's *Wissenschaftslehre*, and Goethe's *Meister*, these are the three representative tendencies of our age'.

'Tendency'? 'Age'? In the light of what I have so far established two very un-Goethean words. But obviously there lurked behind Goethe's theoretical and practical flight into the unconscious of sheer timelessness, or into a tranquil recollection of antiquity, some element which made him, the timeless one, capable —

paradoxically enough — of being hailed as preeminently the artist of the age, its poet *par excellence*. How did his profound impulse to conceal himself, to guard dark areas now being probed by the search-light of Schiller's analytical intellect, respond to the challenge?

The Response: Covert Confessions

Looking back on his relationship with Schiller, Goethe told Eckermann on 14 November 1823:

> It was not his way to proceed unconsciously and as it were instinctively. He had to reflect on everything he did. Which is why he couldn't refrain from talking about his poetic projects, and did in fact discuss all his later plays with me, scene by scene. I, by contrast, could never talk with anybody about my poetic plans; not even with Schiller. It was entirely against my nature. I carried them about with me without saying a word; and it was rare for anyone to learn anything of them until they were completed.

These remarks, uttered retrospectively and not without a touch of malice after a quarter of a century, do not in fact correspond to what actually went on between him and Schiller in the 1790s, when he was sending him *Wilhelm Meister* in instalments, with requests for detailed criticism, and from whom at a crucial moment in the continuation of *Faust* he sought artistic understanding and support. Since Schiller, for all his devotion, would have responded negatively to even the slightest sign of overt withdrawal into privacy, we have to look for the method rather than the manner in Goethe's silences: for a quite consciously calculated form of oblique artistic utterance which had in fact captivated Schiller for over a decade despite his own addiction to defining and formulating. The precisely identifiable 'stations' of this confessional silence may explain why Schlegel thought he had found in this so untimely Goethe the true poet of the new epoch, of the Modern age.

As we have seen, Goethe's first response to Schiller's letter betrayed a characteristic mixture of gratitude and confession; a confession harking back to the darker areas of his own consciousness. What is missing is any attempt at a systematic reply to Schiller's personal and theoretical assault — and were it only in the matter of intellectual substance. After several meetings following on their first epistolary exchanges — during which Goethe's ideas obviously had an intense, but also confusing, effect upon Schiller — Goethe began to accept Schiller's explanatory 'model' of two very different types of mind united by a common interest. True, a certain distance vis-à-vis arguments based on transcendental philosophy made itself felt from the start, and would continue to be a mark of their relationship: Goethe will go on pretending not to understand how a statement about beauty is 'really' only a statement about the form of our own perception when faced with beauty; and will continue to deflect the conversation away from analysis of our forms of seeing and knowing towards the objects of art itself. To this extent his conciliatory answer — that they both had 'a like interest in significant objects' — actually points to the very nerve of the difference between them: to the immediacy of Goethe's own relation to what he calls 'Gegen-stände'. For the time being, however, these contradictions are veiled by the enthusiasm with which they embarked on their several and joint projects in the field of education through art, heralded by the first instalment of Schiller's treatise *On the Aesthetic Education of Man: In a Series of Letters*. In the ninth of these he sketches what was generally taken to be a portrait of Goethe, at the same time providing an Idealist explanation for his 'timeless' quality:

> The artist is indeed the child of his age; but woe to him if he is at the same time its ward or, worse still, its minion. Let some beneficent deity snatch the suckling betimes from his mother's breast, nourish him with the milk of a better age, and suffer him to come to maturity under a distant, a Grecian sky. Then, when he has become a man, let him return, a stranger, to his own century; not, however, to gladden it by his appearance but, terrible as Agamemnon's son, to cleanse and purify it. His themes he will indeed take from the present; but his form he will borrow from a nobler time, nay, from beyond time altogether . . .

Goethe himself took this to refer to his own return to Weimar

from Rome as a purifying-avenging Orestes figure. There's still
room for scholarly dispute about this. But what meanwhile
remains theoretically relevant in Schiller's text is a concept of time
which comes very close indeed to Goethe's own. The point at
issue between them cannot therefore be due to their differing
view of time itself. It must be something *consequent upon* Goethe's
view of time. And this must surely be that playing off of 'objects'
vis-à-vis 'reflection' which had been apparent from the start of
their friendship. Schiller's lively participation in the progress of
Wilhelm Meister during 1795/6, like Goethe's own delighted if brief
replies, shew just how much he did — contrary to later recollections
— allow Schiller at the zenith of their exchanges to share in his
creative process and literary products. And down to the smallest
details! What he in fact did was to respond to Schiller's analytical
criticism of art and the artist by shifting his ground to technical
particulars of craft and the craftsman.

The first clear sign of a more distanced attitude, of a relativization
of Schiller's theoretical engagement in work in progress, is to be
found in the letter Goethe wrote on receipt of *Naive and Sentimental
Poetry*. Instead of going into the substance of this bold attempt at
an entirely new theory, and trying to match Schiller's own
ungrudging concentration and commitment when the boot was
on the other foot, he simply writes — not without a touch of
sophisticated coquetry:

> Since your theory puts me in such a good light, it's only
> natural that I should applaud its principles, and approve
> the conclusions you draw. I might have less confidence in
> them had I not from the start been polemically inclined
> towards your views on the subject. For you are not
> unaware that out of all too great love for the poetry of the
> Ancients I have often been unjust to the Moderns.
> According to your theory I can only become at one with
> myself when I no longer need to chide that which, under
> certain conditions, I was led by an irresistible urge to
> produce.   (29 November 1795)

In other words: Goethe retracts his earlier rejection of modern
poetry, not from theoretical conversion or conviction, but from
purely personal motives that he freely acknowledges. In a sense
he stands Schiller's analysis on its head: this first theoretical essay

on the essential self-reflectiveness of the modern writer, which in
itself he already positively admires, turns ironically enough as he
reads into a sanction of his own misgivings about self-reflection
and theorizing — and into an invitation to surrender to them.
Presumably Schiller's ideas appealed to him because they seemed
above all to legitimize his right *not* to continue the debate on such
heights of critical theory. And on 5 July 1796 he reiterates his
modesty in matters theoretical, offering in response to Schiller's
retrospective analysis of all eight Books of *Wilhelm Meisters Lehrjahre*
this brief and perfunctory comment:

> . . . and now, in the midst of my own very down-to-earth
> avocations you surprise me with two letters which, like
> voices from another world, I am only privileged to listen
> in to. Do please go on revivifying and encouraging me!

The next day he confirms the influence Schiller has had upon the
final form of his novel, and reverts yet again to his own
'unconscious' way of doing things:

> . . . and I feel that even if I were in a state of utter
> composure I would have no reflections of my own to
> return for yours. What you tell me will have to become,
> both as a whole and in all its parts, effective within me in a
> practical way. Go on, please, making me acquainted with
> my own work . . .

If the addressee were not Schiller one might be tempted to read
out of this last sentence one of those ironic put-downs that
creators are wont to administer to critics.

Up to this point Goethe's reservations about reflecting on his
own creative processes have had, so to speak, only negative
application: they have, whether given prominence or taken tacitly
for granted, been treated as a deficit, something lacking in his own
nature. As a result, the quite un- and a-historical image of the
unconsciously creating genius has, right down to the present day,
hardened into a graven image. Whereas Schiller, architect and
prime mover of this image, never intended it to be interpreted
typologically, but only in the new, historico-dialectical, sense.
And even for Goethe himself it was not at bottom a question of
some typological antithesis between theoretical and un-theoretical;
between the conscious and the unconscious artist. Rather about

the much more specific issue of the extent to which our single and simple, in the sense of unanalysed, view of objects — of those 'Gegen-stände' he was forever talking about — could be no less immediately seized upon and used by the poetic, the artistic imagination. Schiller had doubted this. But until now, in the middle nineties, Goethe never had. He had endorsed and celebrated it. And it is only now, when in his letter of 8 July 1796 Schiller criticizes the accidental and contingent nature of the events and motives of Goethe's novel — their vagueness, despite all affectionate detail, when measured against the 'idea' of the whole — that Goethe in reply offers the first positive characterization of his own arcane procedures amd reticences: his refusal not to take seriously things in and for themselves; his area of ultimate retreat into which Schiller is unable to follow him.

> I beg you not to cease from your endeavour to drive me out of — and, I'd be inclined to say, beyond — my own limitations. My great failing, as you so rightly discern, springs from my innermost nature: from a certain addiction to the real, by an indulgence of which I find it convenient to shift my doings as well as my writings, indeed my very existence, out of sight of men's eyes. That's why I like travelling incognito, choosing ordinary rather than fine clothes; or when talking to strangers or mere acquaintances prefer the insignificant topic or less significant expression; make myself seem even more frivolous than I am — and thus, so to speak, interpose me between my self and the appearance of myself.
>
> (9 July 1796)

Thus was the deficit in his own nature turned into an asset: the asset of primogeniture. This is the letter (of all those many letters) which contains the deepest, the most substantial explanation of the abstinence he henceforth imposed upon himself in respect of utterances about his own creativity and methods of working. The burden of argument is now no longer left to Schiller the theoretician. From now on the opposing power is something no less fundamental: 'der realistiche Tic' which Goethe has acknowledged and named. It now becomes increasingly clear where Goethe is not disposed to follow. Where he neither can — nor will. Never, that is, to the point where poetic 'objects' are so consciously known and contrived that they promptly interpret themselves as it were, and thus function as 'idea'. Goethe's 'realistischer Tic' is in sum no mere stylistic adornment; not a formal failure either; nor a structural weakness in the economy of the work as a whole. His real secret, one might say, is the understating of the idea through things: through his obstinate attachment to objects. That he was finally able to formulate this is due to Schiller's challenge, which at this point reached the limits of its efficacy. On 10 August 1796 there followed, almost as an aside, a clear indication that Goethe is no longer willing to be interrogated or put right about his 'realistischer Tic':

> My novel too is shewing signs of life again. I have in my own peculiar way been able to give body to your ideas. Whether you will recognize such spiritual beings in this their earthy form I do not know. I'm almost inclined to send it to press without shewing you any more. Because of the difference in our two natures it can never meet all your requirements.

Here Goethe makes clear that there can, with respect, be no congruence between 'spiritual beings' and 'earthy forms'; that he can no longer take account of this inherent 'mismatch'; and that he will in future not even try. From now on Goethe was ready to engage with Schiller in the most detailed debate about theories of art; to confront him with problems arising from the enormous amount of material he had gathered for his *Faust*; or to tangle with him in discussions about the genres — epic, dramatic etc. But never again did he allow him such intensive closeness as during their correspondence about *Wilhelm Meister*. After another year, in which Goethe's object-oriented realism received further justification, there followed the laconic statement, in a letter of 30 December 1797: 'Theoretical reflections cannot entertain me much longer; I must get back to work'.

What occasioned this gradual cooling off is no longer of interest today if looked at from a psycho-typological point of view. But it is of great interest in respect of what Goethe conceived as a poetic subject ('Gegen-stand'). As one of the characters in his *Unterhaltungen deutscher Ausgewanderten* puts it: 'every phenomenon, like every fact, has to be of interest in itself' (HA, VI, 161). And it is in these years of the mid-1790s that Goethe himself starts to put the stamp of 'classical' upon that object-oriented aesthetic he'd been inclined to from the start. Its focus is the priority of the object within the subject-object relation. Or, as he put it in the entry of his *Italian Journey* dated 17 September 1786 from Verona: 'I did not embark upon this wondrous journey in order to delude myself, but in order to learn about myself through attention to objects.' The whole programme of a classical theory of art, one might say, based as it was upon actual acquaintance with classical antiquity, was only able to o'erleap objections to its neglect of epochs, periods, and the differences between them, because Goethe — like no other of his contemporaries — was fascinated by objects, themes, motifs, subject-matter. It is this that gives his contribution to the exchanges with Schiller on subjects suitable for epic treatment the air of some staid conserver or restorer of antiques. It was an air which was bound to attract to itself — as the response to his *Hermann und Dorothea* clearly shews — the sort of academic classicism in which the objects of art and nature become something of a fetish and promote a ritual invocation of the 'objectivity' of ancient truths, with 'apt' quotations from his still profoundly misunderstood poem 'Vermächtnis' always ready to hand — 'Das alte Wahre, fass es an!' — and a consequent neglect, where not outright disparagement, of the historical time-factor and modern subjectivity. If Goethe himself did not take the dead-end way of such ossifying classicism, but instead completed both Parts of his *Faust*, it was precisely because his 'realistischer Tic', his attachment to the real, to the priority of objects, underwent a quite specific metamorphosis. It is this that helps towards an understanding of the question I've posed: How was it that Goethe, the most a-temporal of spirits, should nevertheless have been acclaimed by Friedrich Schlegel as *the* poet of the age?

In reply to Goethe's letter of 16 August 1797 Schiller put a definite if provocative stop to quesions about the inherent poeticness of any particular subject ('Gegenstand'). It is not the theme itself, but the perceiving mind that makes poetry:

> You speak as though everything depended on the subject ('Gegenstand'). With this I cannot agree. True, the theme chosen must have inherent *significance*, just as a 'poetic' object must itself *be* something. But in the final analysis it all depends on the percipient, on his psyche: on whether

this object is significant to *him*. Which is why I think that we must look for the source of emptiness or fulness of import in the subject rather than the object.

Although Goethe never gave up defending 'things', in all their thusness and contingency, against the subject-oriented priorities of Transcendental Idealism (see his letter of 6 January 1798), he nevertheless modified his position of 'stubborn Realist'. And as early as 1796, in a letter to F.H. Jacobi of 17 October, he underlined the fact that the perceiving subject must strive 'to apprehend objects with as little distortion, and as fully, as possible'. Clearly Schiller's categorical insistence on the subject-oriented significance of objects had already been anticipated by Goethe in a significant way. But at the same time — and this is what Schiller failed to understand — in a way which forced him to find an entirely new foundation for justifying his own kind of object-orientation.

What exactly had happened? In that same letter of 16 August 1797, to whose theoretical standpoint Schiller responded with such negative provocation, Goethe had also told him of a recent object-oriented experience which had engaged him deeply. There are, he wrote, 'certain objects' which exude 'a sort of "sentimentality" for our feeling'. These objects are not necessarily poetic in themselves; the 'poetic mood and mode' must therefore stem from our own 'being'. Objects having such an effect he would be inclined to call 'symbolic'. They are cases which stand for many others as representative of some characteristic manifold of experience. Such 'eminente Fälle', as he called them, do not rate the status of a 'poetic form'. But an 'ideal form' — human form raised to a higher power — that is something that can rightly be attributed to them. As an example he offers the Rossmarkt where he's put up during his stay in Frankfurt, and the spot once occupied by his grandfather's house and garden but now, since the bombardment, converted by enterprising men into a market-place. What he found 'symbolic' in such locations, or 'objects', was that they 'represented' an economic change also taking place in thousands of other cases. Let's make no mistake about it: Goethe is no longer even attempting to derive the 'sense' of such objects from their immediate impact upon our senses, from their sheer 'poetic' valency. Rather from our apprehension of their historic transformation in the light of new economic significances. It is not possible to explore here to what extent this newly discovered quality in an 'object' unpoetic in itself can be adequately accounted for by any such concept as the 'symbol'. Or whether, as Heinz Schaffer has argued, the term allegory would not be more appropriate, a concept he thinks Goethe was moving towards.[5] It is enough to recognize that, in the course of having a socio-historical experience, Goethe apprehends significances in 'objects' un-poetic in themselves. Schiller's characteristic lack of understanding throws light on Goethe's discovery: the special quality of the 'object' does not after all reside in the general reflective structure of the apprehending psyche! Schiller's epistemological idealism was not in effect adequate to Goethe's grasp of socio-historical sensibility. And yet it was after all he — Schiller — who, on 23 June 1797, had first introduced into their correspondence the concept of 'symbolic significance' in connection with the Faust-theme. What he understood by it was however only the formal need for some 'ideal' import. And, irritated that Goethe had once again caught him napping by coming up with a new project, namely his old Faust-theme, and profoundly mistrustful of his joy in this rediscovered subject/object, he categorically decreed:

> precisely because this old legend tends towards formlessness and theatrical clap-trap one cannot stop short with the theme itself, but must let oneself be led on to its underlying ideas. In short: the challenges presented are philosophic as well as poetic; and the very nature of the theme will impose a philosophical treatment whether you like it or not. In other words: your imagination will have to accommodate itself to the service of a rational idea.

From which we see that what 'symbolic' means for Schiller is nothing more than the transcendental structure of individual phenomena. Whereas for Goethe it was only through the concept of symbol that the object itself might be 'saved' in all its factual thusness. Thanks to his 'realistic quirk' he had seen himself branded as adherent of an 'empiricism' whose crude, un-poetic, character deeply disturbed and depressed him during the first half of the 1790s. That journey of 1797, which led him back to

Weimar via his Frankfurt beginnings, opened up to him a world which, by contrast with his journey to Italy, seemed all set to turn into something radically prosaic. And indeed in his first letters from his birthplace he stresses his aversion to the 'empirical spread' which travelling brings. Though it may as a whole, and in the longer term, have a beneficial effect, the impression of so many 'empirical details' is unpleasant (12 August 1797); one longs for the tranquillity of recollection ('Besonnenheit'); it is now that he begins to complain of his failure to perceive things in a way which would have merited an epigram (27 December 1797). But whereas Schiller, operating with the categories of Idealist philosophy, thought he had disposed of such nagging reflections by directing Goethe's attention to the concept of 'gemeiner Empirismus', which takes the 'reality' of objects for granted (or, like Dr Johnson, claims to have demonstrated it by bashing a foot against a stone!) as opposed to a 'Transcendental empiricism' which reckons with the mind of the perceiving subject (19 January 1798), Goethe himself went on worrying away at the problem posed for poets by objects which are in themselves totally devoid of anything 'poetic'. It was his unceasing dialogue with objects themselves which led Goethe to *his* notion of the symbol. And we should note that it's not the term that's important, but his continuing attachment to 'real' things. After he had grappled with what, in his letter to Schiller of 17 August 1797, he called 'the hydra-headed concept of empiricism', he does not disqualify any objects from meriting his own brand of 'zarte Empirie', but simply gives this new concept an historical habitation and a name.

We are now in a position to draw the first of our paradoxical conclusions. It was precisely Goethe's a-historical attachment to 'real' objects that eventually brought him to an understanding of the overt and covert changes taking place in the historical age in which he lived. This awareness he derived, as he always had done, from the objects towards which he directed that 'undistorting gaze' which had originally compelled Schiller's attention. And he was able to go on deriving it from them even when they no longer offered themselves as objects for purely poetic contemplation as they had done when he was in Italy. Under the shock he experienced when, coming again — in violent times — to his own birthplace, one of the Free Cities of the old Holy Roman Empire and now more than most caught up in radically new economic change, he at first took refuge in his own subjective need for 'reflection' ('Besonnenheit'). But, unlike Schiller, he did not protect himself by recourse to Idealist, let alone Dialectical, methods of 'saving by abolishing' the object perceived. Instead he developed his own version of sophisticated or 'sceptical' Realism (12 August 1797). In pursuit of this he insists on discovering the symbolic content of such objects as engage his attention by trying to penetrate to their depths 'in the very moment, in the very place' at which he finds them; in order, as he puts it, to 'practise' this uncovering of the dignity of things — and quite especially to pursue this when they and their context are unfamiliar (16 August 1797). The decisive factor for him is thus not the 'Transcendental Argument' of the subjectivity of the percipient; but the objectivity of things in their local and temporal habitation. We should note that a new dimension has thus been added; a dimension which the classical 'objects' of the period between his Italian Journey and his theory of the Epic did not possess: a significance, namely, not necessarily discoverable by attention to the here and now, to the present context of objects, but — potentially at least — to their future. From this there follow two new conditions of object-relatedness:

1   a time-reflecting factor hitherto lacking in Goethe's conception of objects. This is however, for the time being, construed as a property possessed as a specific mystery by the specific object in its specific location. Significances which do not immediately yield their secret may yet imply a promise for the future; that is to say, a continuing reflection in the perspective of time. The objects themselves nevertheless remain — and all the more in spite of this — unassailably 'there', and present to our senses;

2   the recourse to a 'sense' which does not, as formerly, derive directly from Goethe's intent contemplation of a localized object, but has nevertheless its own sort of complexity. This manifold of meaning still obtains even when based on exact dates, social and economic changes etc. For such interrelated factors presuppose, not merely the 'representative' nature of the object, but the effect of memory in the perceiving subject: our recollection of

former ages. This implies that the object is not just susceptible of one, unambiguous, interpretation: it remains open to many ways of seeing and feeling it. Thus even 'representativeness' does not of itself imply a logical relation of 'object' to some distinguishable 'idea' or 'meaning'. On the contrary: it implies that which it has in common with other localities and places.

In other words: what Goethe henceforth experiences in specific objects — and what had hitherto been hidden from him — was their specifically historical dimension. And this was an insight — the first clear insight — heralding Modernism.

And so we come to our closing paradoxical conclusion. It was through a place of purely private significance to him — the changes wrought by economic factors in the area surrounding his grandparents' home — that Goethe first came to recognize this temporal nature of all objects. Thus his visit to Frankfurt in August 1797 represents an eminently significant 'station' in his inner biography. Instead of recording this quite personally momentous re-encounter directly, he conceals it behind references to 'objects' and their changing locality. He speaks not of himself but of them. This 'masking' of himself has rarely been understood by his compatriots, Schiller not excepted. And it may have required the delicacy of perception, independence of mind, and sovereign distance of a young Englishman — fictitious though he may be — to put a finger on this paradox and call it by nature and by name. On the obligatory visit to Goethe during his Grand Tour the twenty-four-year-old Sir Andrew Marbot, fantasy figure of Wolfgang Hildesheimer, formulated his impression of the seventy-five-year-old as follows:

> He seemed to me far greater than his works, at any rate those known to me. What radiates from him is the sense of a man in whom Nature has concentrated all her forces as in one she has singled out among mortals to be the jewel mediating between her and the rest of mankind. He sees more truly than the rest of us — though some phenomena he misinterprets. He's wrong in his view of some things — but one hestitates to disagree, because even as he speaks many things shift into a new light. He is a work of art in himself — but then, one may ask: How

does a work of art bring forth works of art? And if so, how is it possible to judge them without reference back to the man who created them? Even his graciousness has a sort of condescension — which yet seems perfectly natural; for if such a great man, who obviously knows his own stature and worth, were to stoop to false modesty, we should deem it an intolerable misjudgment, and hence a sort of coquetry. His greatness manifests itself not least in the fact that he never speaks of himself. Of everything else — just as he is *in* everything else. Yet in speaking of everything else he also speaks about himself.[6]

Marbot's letter presents in the form of personal document what by means of theoretical analysis can be discovered from the Goethe-Schiller correspondence. It's all there: the quite unusual attentiveness to what is to be observed; the degree of object-relatedness — even to the point where the perceiving subject merges with the object perceived. But this form of silence — of reticence, discretion, of the left-unsaid — is certainly the proudest, maybe even the noblest, way of talking about oneself. This is the point of his much quoted, and even more misunderstood, statement in *Dichtung und Wahrheit* (HA, IX, 283) that all his works were but fragments of a 'Great Confession'. The fact that his works were rooted in a nature which threw him perpetually from one extreme to the other may be interpreted as the bodily 'cause' of the works of his imagination.

It is this 'bodiliness' of his thoughts that, in the last analysis, outweighed his former neglect of temporality, and prevented the danger of any sort of a-historical classicizing in his ardent exploration of the objects of art and nature. Emil Staiger's hypothesis that the 'timeless moment' is the characteristic form of Goethe's imagination is one we can no longer go along with. Far more fundamental than any such a-historical moment was Goethe's own bodily consciousness of his own 'nature': a nature which from the start had led him to a contemplation and observation of 'objects'. Whether Friedrich Schlegel's well-known dictum about 'the three great tendencies of the age' is valid or not; or whether a measure of distance towards the theory of self-reflection inclines us to the diametrically opposite view — the decisive factor was in the end Goethe's own fine, discriminating perception when confronted by quite ordinary things. Things he named by their quite ordinary names[7] — thereby making them, as the young today in the wisdom of their a-historical innocence would have it, 'magic'. What in the last resort was the decisive criterion for Goethe was not the Romantics' cult of suffering, but the body and its pains. It was a criterion which took a huge leap over the Dialectical Philosophy of History, no less than over the self-reflectiveness of Transcendental Idealism, to come to rest — maybe for the last time — on 'saving' simple things for a modern spirit beyond Modernism.

Translated from the German by Elizabeth M. Wilkinson.

Notes to Covert Confessions: The Tension between Goethe and Schiller

[*Translator's Note:* At some points, especially on pp. 100-06, English — like French — usage requires 'subject' for *Gegenstand*, otherwise consistently rendered as 'object'. Goethe and Schiller were well aware of this, but relied on context rather than the introduction of another term to make their meaning clear. Readers are referred to the Glossary of our bilingual edition of Schiller's *Aesthetic Education of Man* (Oxford University Press, 1967), pp 312f. Though now out of print, a paperback facsimile was promised for the autumn.]

1.   *Euphorion*, 66 (1972), 174f. In his letter to Goethe, Schiller is not yet operating with the terms 'naive' and 'sentimental'. Nor do the terms 'intuition' and 'analysis' yet serve in their place, as Szondi suggests they might well do in Schiller's treatise itself. But early signs of the influence of contemporary history of philosophy are none the less evident in this challenging letter.

2.   Their disunity was noted by Karl Schmid in his Introduction to the Goethe-Schiller Correspondence in GA, XX (1950). See also Georg Lukács, 'Der Briefwechsel zwischen Schiller und Goethe', in *Deutsche Literatur in zwei Jahrhunderten* (Vienna and Berlin, 1964), pp. 96f.; Wilkinson and Willoughby, Schiller's *Aesthetic Education of Man*, ed. cit., pp. xxxv-xlii; and Emil Staiger, 'Fruchtbare Missverständnisse Goethes und Schillers', in *Spätzeit. Studien zur Deutschen Literatur* (Zurich

and Munich, 1973), pp. 52f. Ilse Graham, by contrast, stresses their unity: ' "Zweiheit in Einklang". Der Briefwechsel zwischen Schiller und Goethe', *Goethe Jahrbuch*, 95 (1978), 37f.

3. See, for instance, H.R. Jauss, *Literaturgeschichte als Provokation* (Frankfurt am Main, 1970), pp. 95f.

4. See Peter Pfaff, 'Das Horen-Märchen. Eine Replique Goethes auf Schillers Briefe über die ästhetische Erziehung', in *Geist und Zeichen. Festschrift für Arthur Henkel* (Heidelberg, 1977).

5. *Faust Zweiter Teil. Die Allegorie des 19. Jahrhunderts* (Stuttgart, 1981), pp. 13–28.

6. Quoted from Wolfgang Hildesheimer, *Marbot. Eine Biographie* (Frankfurt am Main, 1981), pp. 11f.

7. Cf. L.A. Willoughby, 'On the Study of Goethe's Imagery' (1949); reprinted in *Goethe. Poet and Thinker*, pp. 122f.

Goethe and Happiness   T.J. Reed

> Il faut estendre la joye, mais retrencher
> autant qu'on peut la tristesse.
>
> Montaigne, *De la vanité*

World-historical individuals, Hegel tells us in the Introduction to his *Lectures on the Philosophy of History,* are never happy. In his scheme of things, they are too busy being the instruments through which the World Spirit realizes itself in history. Beside this function, individual happiness —like most individual human claims for Hegel — is a trivial matter.

I have chosen to collect here a few celebratory thoughts around the counter-proposition that Goethe — a 'world-historical individual' if anyone in German literature is —was in fact happy: that his happiness was, and is, not at all trivial but something of great and general significance; that if he had a world-historical mission at all, it lay precisely in being happy, and in the mode of his happiness.

There would probably not be much dissent from the statement that Goethe had a happy life. Always excepting some of his own more morose statements in old age, such as that to Eckermann, on 27 January 1824, that in all his seventy-five years he had not enjoyed more than four weeks' 'eigentliches Behagen'. He enjoyed success and eminence, he fulfilled his talents in a wide range of pursuits, he interacted with the best men of his day and had the satisfaction of being exhaustively understood by at least one of them; he felt at home in a world that seemed to him comprehensible, he achieved a high degree of inner harmony and of harmony with his environment. By the standard of what a man of letters in eighteenth-century Germany could expect, he was immensely fortunate.

In so far as his good fortune was external and social, it has been held against him by periods, our own especially, which prefer their cultural heroes to be the adversaries of society, its critics or outcasts. Of which more later. But his happiness was not only, and not primarily, external and social. Its development was essentially independent of society, which gave it little direct nourishment; rather, the space for it to develop in had to be positively wrested from society. And what was there to develop was something personal and given, a capacity present from the first in Goethe's nature. It is one of the qualities that make his youthful writing a revolution.

The poetry most obviously. This is familiar ground, but it can never be sufficiently celebrated. 'Mailied', for example, is happiness exuberant and unalloyed, bursting forth in the most direct way. The poetic voice is uninhibited by previous poetic convention: 'a man speaking to men', in Wordsworth's phrase, through simple stanzas which seem the necessary reflex of an overflowing emotion. It is not only the simplicity that makes it a new poetry, but the sense of immediately perceived reality. 'Happiness' is not a set theme for the sort of poetic reflections typical of the eighteenth century, but an immediate intuition; the things he perceives about him — sun, fields, blossoms, birdsong — are not a rhetorical elaboration of the idea 'I am happy', which is never expressly stated, but the realities which inspire the mood and express it in the act of being named. Happiness — and this is a first sign of its place in Goethe's mental life — is not self-absorbed; it absorbs and orders the observable world.

Happiness is also the substance of 'Willkommen und Abschied'. Long before the closing exclamations accept love as high good fortune whatever its pains — 'Und doch, welch Glück, geliebt zu werden,/Und lieben, Götter, welch ein Glück!' — the whole poem has been carried along by it. The power of the opening, 'Es schlug mein Herz, geschwind zu Pferde!', is its sense of a happy impulse to set out through night and nature and find its confirmation and renewal at the journey's end. The gothic gloom of clouds and winds and moon and imagined monsters is half-humorous, no real threat to a man who has the happiness of love burning in him: 'Mein Geist war ein verzehrend Feuer,/Mein ganzes Herz zerfloss in Glut!' Again the effect is simple. It comes from forthright statement in effortlessly ordered massive stanzas; once more in contrast to what had gone before in the eighteenth century, where poetic power had been bought (by Klopstock) at the price of formal and verbal contortion and a strenuously sought-after sublimity.

To complete an early trilogy of happiness (I omit 'Ganymed', which is about not just happiness but ecstasy) there is 'Auf dem See'. Two possible forms of happiness compete. There is what the present moment offers, invigoration at the opening of the poem and serenity at the close; and there are the 'goldne Träume' of a recent past to which the middle quatrain harks back, and which implicitly claim that only their world can provide 'Lieb und Leben'. Even without knowing the biographical background, we might guess it is the social world that calls the poet back from his benevolent natural setting, and that the decision the poem enacts turns on the different meaning and value of 'love and life' in a social and a natural context. The line 'Hier auch Lieb und Leben ist' defiantly opts for nature rather than society, seeing 'love and life' in all the things about him which the final octet registers: the sun on the lake surface, the mist shrouding the mountains, the morning breeze, the sheltered bay. They reach a gentle climax in the phenomena of reflection and maturing —'Und im See bespiegelt/Sich die reifende Frucht' — which suggest that his experiences share an identical structure with the processes of nature. He is, as the opening lines so vigorously showed him to be (especially in the original version) nature's child indeed. The decision where he truly belonged was scarcely his to take.

Though this is as rich and complex as any poem Goethe wrote, it grows again from simple roots. Whatever we admire — the interweaving of literal and symbolic meanings, or the last octet's unforced *exemplificatio,* which surpasses any deliberate baroque effect, or the precise aptness of the final three-part structure to the movement of moods it expresses — everything flows directly from a man stating, questioning, and emphatically restating his happiness and the overwhelming reasons for it. A man, of course, whose capacity for giving a voice to individual experience seems to have been innate, and sometimes (as here) instantaneous; and a man who had an unshakable trust in the authority of his own

physical, earthly being against all doubts and dogmas. In a letter
to J.C. Lavater of 28 October 1779 he called himself 'ein sehr
irdischer Mensch . . . aus der Wahrheit der fünf Sinne', for whom
the highest joy had been summed up five years earlier to his
friend Schönborn in the eloquent words 'das Wohnen in sich
selbst' (8 June 1774). In both cases he was contrasting his own
with Lavater's Christian temper of mind. Seen by such a man, the
world appears in a new light. It is the reverse of the story of the
emperor's new clothes. It took naivety to see and say what *was*
there, just as it took a child to say what wasn't. The real world, and
the experience of living in it as a sentient and sensuous being, only
needed someone who would perceive precisely, respond with
exhilaration, and state the obvious. What *was* then obvious was
that the world was a good place and that experience within it and
of it were good and valuable things. Happiness was possible and
so was its expression. We do well to hang on to this (itself very
obvious) point. For the writer as a happy man is very nearly a lost
concept. Nor was the happiness merely a matter of chance or
episodic: the poetic record of immediate happy experience is
complemented by other poems that suggest the systematic
benevolence of the world — of gods, or God, or Fate, or an
indwelling personal genius. Poems such as 'Eis-Lebens-Lied',
'Wandrers Sturmlied', 'An Schwager Kronos', or 'Seefahrt'. These
turn perceptions into allegory; but the allegory of a purely
personal security, resting on that same sense of physical contact
with what is real.

Was all this so much of an achievement? The historian of ideas
will say that the notion of a harmonious universe and of man in
harmony with it is an eighteenth-century commonplace, almost
the orthodoxy of the age, and he will quote us a fistful of thinkers.
But it is, precisely, a *notion*, and he will quote *thinkers*. Where do we
find the happy man who ought to bear out their doctrines? Not in
the thinkers' writings — that isn't something philosophical works
can easily body forth (though David Hume's tone may suggest
it — but he is a very different sort of philosopher); and in any case
the arguments with which they support the thesis often turn out to
be tentative and provisional, revealing a gap in conviction which
had to be bridged by faith. But nor do we find the happy man in
earlier eighteenth-century poets, who seem unable to escape into
what Goethe significantly calls the 'freie Welt'; or who, if they

seem about to, as Brockes sometimes does, will suddenly scuttle back into the shell of religious orthodoxy and revert to inter-preting the empirical world as a teleological pattern-book. Not until Goethe's early work is the happy man available for our inspection, breathing, perceiving, feeling, living in nature as distinct from reflecting on it, and convincing us that this is both a zestful and a normal mode of being.

So Goethe hardly seems a derivate of eighteenth-century official optimism, but almost more a historical coincidence, the full-blooded reality which comes as if to mock the age's struggle to find the world acceptable. Of course, we may hear echoes of systems and sources in what he writes. For example, the con-fidence in his fate, the recurrent sense of a privileged destiny in his poems and letters, recalls Pietism and its belief in a personal providence; and we might find a prototype for such utterances in his own pietist days in 1769 when he records the moments 'wenn ich stille ganz stille binn, und alles Gute fühle was aus der ewigen Quelle auf mich geflossen ist' (to Langer, 17 January 1769). But if we think of the darker side to Pietism, or for that matter to any version of Christian belief, the question is whether it didn't take the particular set of Goethe's mind, a prior talent for happiness, to make from it such a serene private vision. To put it at its simplest: if Pietism gave him his trust in destiny, why did it give him no sense of sin, no disposition to repent of his being and doing, no doubts of the value of earthly fulfilment? As he wrote to Auguste von Stolberg on 16 September 1775, it was pointless 'uns aufs ewige Leben [zu] vertrösten. Hier noch müssen wir glücklich seyn'.

In philosophy much the same applies. Here there is an influence that Goethe declares in the strongest terms: 'Spinoza, der entschieden auf mich wirkte und auf meine ganze Denkweise so grossen Einfluss haben sollte' (HA, X, 35). But the mechanics of the influence are intriguing. We notice that Goethe twice, in separate passages of *Dichtung und Wahrheit,* hedges his statement and suggests he may have read things into the philosopher (HA, X, 35 and 78). From this, and from what he says about the fundamental differences underlying their 'notwendige Wahlver-wandtschaft', it would be easy to construct the customary argument in favour of poetry and in relative disparagement of its sources in 'graue Theorie'. But more interesting than this is to see how powerfully Goethe's own *intellectual* conceptions are at work as he assimilates Spinoza, so that a snippet of a not very significant phrase from the *Ethics* is melted down and crucially reshaped by a fire that is already furiously burning.

In 1786, with Goethe getting ever deeper into science, he reads Spinoza again. He sees his own practice of 'schauen' reflected in the concept of 'scientia intuitiva', which Spinoza defines (and Goethe quotes him) as 'a mode of knowledge proceeding from an adequate idea of the formal essence of certain attributes of God to an adequate knowledge of the essence of things' (to Jacobi, 5 May 1786).[1] This, Goethe says, fills him with the courage to devote his whole life to the contemplation of things, of whose 'formal essence' (he repeats Spinoza's Latin phrase) he hopes to gain at least a partial 'adequate idea'. The enthusiasm seems a bit disproportionate to the dry scholastic language of attributes and essences. What after all is an essence? In Spinoza's usage, something colourless enough; it is 'that which, when granted, necessarily involves the granting of the thing and which, when removed, necessarily involves the removal of the thing' (*Ethics* II, Definition II). Two months later Goethe almost has the 'Urpflanze' in his grasp. And on 9 July — still before his secretive flight to Italy — he shares his excitement with Charlotte von Stein:

> Es zwingt sich mir alles auf, ich sinne nicht mehr drüber, es kommt mir alles entgegen und das ungeheure Reich simplificirt sich mir in der Seele, dass ich bald die schwerste Aufgabe gleich weglesen kann. Wenn ich nur jemanden (*sic*) den Blick und die Freude mittheilen könnte, es ist aber nicht möglich. Und es ist kein Traum keine Phantasie; es ist ein Gewahrwerden der wesentlichen Form, mit der die Natur gleichsam nur immer spielt und spielend das manigfaltige Leben hervorbringt.

That is the 'Urpflanze' in all but name: the shape present to Goethe's eye in every plant, the simple origin of all species that nature in her infinite variety of play produces. And where is Spinoza? The dry term 'formal essence' has been made to yield an 'essential form' — 'ein Gewahrwerden der wesentlichen Form' — and at a stroke it has become something mobile, flowing, visualizable, like a piece of computer graphics. It is much more than the traditional 'book of nature'. Nature moves before our eyes.

And in tracing the mechanics of an 'influence', to see how little Goethe needed to borrow, we have not moved far from the theme of happiness; for his science is only an extension, a deepening and ordering, of that capacity in the early poems to find the world beautiful and exhilarating and to respond by celebrating its forms and forces. The impulse at the centre remains, appreciative emotion striving to find expression: 'wenn ich nur jemanden den Blick und die Freude mittheilen könnte . . .'.

So it would be difficult to dismiss Goethe's uniquely positive and live perceptions by saying that he merely benefited from an age when happiness and harmony were — even if only in theory — available on tap from authorized sources. Spinoza of course was not even an 'authorized source', but a bête noire of orthodoxy, to whom Goethe like other independent eighteenth-century minds only came 'durch Widerrede' (HA, X, 76). In any case one may doubt whether an age ever existed, outside the imaginings of modern 'Kulturpessimisten', in which culture made coming to terms with life an effortless business. It was surely always a creative achievement. And if Goethe draws on other minds, it is as an eclectic for whom those he called in the *Farbenlehre* the 'echten Menschen aller Zeiten' (HA, XIV, 100) confirm, or can be made to seem to confirm, or can serve as a pretext for uttering, the truths he himself is sure of. This is just as true of his turn to classical sources, which were only fruitful because of the life he brought to them. He may model his verse on Latin elegy and invoke Catullus and Propertius and Ovid as his forerunners in love and poetry, but everything that makes the *Roman Elegies* valuable is new and his. The feeling is quite unlike that of the Roman poets — it is stable, warm, even, not embattled, tortured, cynical. Happiness is possible through the mutual responsiveness of man and woman, just as it was possible in the early poems through the mutual responsiveness of man and landscape. Once again, as there, the obvious is stated with the force of a revelation; shocking therefore to eighteenth-century readers, and — for all the progress of sexual emancipation — rarely equalled since as poetry about fulfilled sexual love in the real world.

But if Goethe's harmony was personal and not derivative, was it perhaps facile? Did it ignore the darker side of existence? Was he an untragic poet? Certainly he was not prepared to be tragic for the sake of it. For Goethe life was too complex to be only tragic, and when situations could be resolved he resolved them. It is worth remembering that, when we speak of other writers' 'tragic vision', we sometimes mean little more than a proclivity to write tragedy in the conventional mould. Still, no reader of *Werther,* or the last scenes of *Faust I*, or the *Wahlverwandtschaften*, or the Philemon and Baucis scenes in *Faust II*, could maintain that Goethe ignored, or in any poetically culpable way avoided, tragedy. He was as continuously aware as any poet that beneficent nature was also an 'ewig verschlingendes, ewig wiederkäuendes Ungeheuer' (*Werther*, Book I, 18 August), an endless ocean of 'Geburt und Grab' (*Faust*, line 504). The gods gave their favourites 'alle Freuden' but also 'alle Schmerzen die unendlichen, ganz' (HA, I, 142). The happiness of the early poems, even, is not the result of having always been gentled along by an unproblematically serene nature. In a review of 1772 in the *Frankfurter Gelehrte Anzeigen* he wrote:

> Überhaupt tut sie das nie, sie härtet vielmehr, Gott sei Dank, ihre echten Kinder gegen die Schmerzen und Übel ab, die sie ihnen unablässig bereitet, so dass wir den den glücklichsten Menschen nennen können, der der Stärkste wäre, dem Übel zu entgegnen, es von sich zu weisen und ihm zum Trutz den Gang seines Willens zu gehen.   (HA, XII, 17)

The affirmation of life in that early declaration has a positively Nietzschean ring of toughness and realism. If happiness was possible, it was not necessarily easy.

It virtually follows that Goethe's happiness was not facile in the sense of being mere hedonistic enjoyment. It lay in responding to diversity, harmonizing what seemed disharmonious, meeting the challenge of the world about him and ultimately of the potential within him, of whose needs and demands he is aware from early on. If this sounds moral in its strenuousness, it is not a general morality in Kant's manner but a purely personal imperative. Typical is a progress-report to his mother of 11 August 1781 comparing the former restrictions of Frankfurt with the trials and tribulations of Weimar, which are proving fruitful for his 'Ausbildung': '. . . . wie könnte ich mir, nach meiner Art zu seyn, einen glücklichern Zustand wünschen, als einen der für mich etwas unendliches hat'. Whatever new qualities it develops in him, there is a practical use for. If all this is also a great strain, it is bearable because voluntary: he knows that at any time he could throw it all over and take horses back to Frankfurt, 'um das notdürftige und Angenehme des Lebens, mit einer unbedingten Ruhe, bey Ihnen wieder zu finden'. The wording hints that the philosophic issues of *Faust* as stated in the 'Prolog im Himmel' — 'des Menschen Tätigkeit' versus 'unbedingte Ruh' — are already there for the formulating; the commitment to ceaseless activity, to 'Streben' rather than 'Genuss', is already of long standing. In talking of Goethe's happiness, we are all the time on Faustian ground. But it is the occasional letter that gives the most immediate sense of Goethe's psychological, even physical need for an outlet in activity. For example he had spoken of the writing of *Götz* as a relief in those same restrictions of Frankfurt (to Salzmann, 28 November 1771): 'denn es ist traurig an einem Ort zu leben wo unsre ganze Wircksamkeit in sich selbst summen muss'. He is a man carrying a very high current.

Italy offered the perfect illustration for all this, because it provided the fullest scope for self-realization in activity. Goethe went to Italy to realize a childhood dream — to that extent, he was yet again carrying his own fulfilment with him. But Italy gave him an immensity of things to assimilate: the art of antiquity and of the Renaissance, and the mediterranean landscapes that had fostered them; an 'Abgrund der Kunst' and 'Abgründe der Natur' (the abyss here is a wholly positive, not as so often in modern usage a pessimistic image) — all this to be seen, understood in its individuality and necessity, and brought together in a single vision of art, nature, history and humanity. So when he writes to Weimar friends that Rome is not all 'Genuss', that the burden of seeing and experiencing is almost too much for him; or when his estimate of the time needed to digest it all escalates in a quick succession of letters from half a year to a year to years to a lifetime, it is not just the tactics of a truant. Far from it. He is working hard; he is indeed the progressive educationist's ideal — the supremely self-motivated student pursuing a course of his own design.

Of course it is enjoyable too. His letters brim over with conscious happiness and renewal. In 1788, at the end of his nearly two years there, he says that it was a paradise, the first time in his life that he had been absolutely happy (to Karl August, 18 March;

to Herder, 5 June); the motto to the *Italienische Reise* later makes it
an Arcadia. It was indeed an idyll; and the contemporary record,
especially the journal of the first few weeks' journeying to Rome
and the unedited letters of the whole stay, can be read as one of the
few absorbing idylls in literature. That is because it is an idyll of
fulfilled activity, not of pastoral escapism; and as such it perfectly
fits Schiller's account in *Naive and Sentimental Poetry* of what a
modern idyll could and should be:

> Ruhe wäre also der herrschende Eindruck dieser
> Dichtungsart, aber Ruhe der Vollendung, nicht der
> Trägheit; eine Ruhe, die aus dem Gleichgewicht nicht
> aus dem Stillstand der Kräfte, die aus der Fülle nicht aus
> der Leerheit fliesst, und von dem Gefühle eines unend-
> lichen Vermögens begleitet wird.

That happiness should in some sense lie in activity is not a
wholly new idea. In his *Nichomachean Ethics* (I, 8) Aristotle calls
happiness 'an activity in accordance with virtue'; and his concept
of 'eudaimonia' is one of worthwhile human pursuits as distinct
from simple gratification.[2] But Goethe's conception is much
more radically dynamic than this. His understanding and practice
of happiness-as-activity is only the tip of a consistent belief that
man and the nature he is part of are process rather than static
being. Plant species are not for Goethe the fixed entities earlier
botanists had held them to be, but stages in a continuum of
change. Nature is not, as she had commonly been seen, a system
but a movement: 'Die Natur hat kein System, sie hat, sie ist Leben
und Folge aus einem unbekannten Zentrum zu einer nicht
erkennbaren Grenze' (HA, XIII, 35). Goethe's Faust, similarly and
for similar reasons, breaks with tradition: instead of craving for
pleasurable states, like his predecessors, he pursues a seemingly
impossible satisfaction that will somehow still keep all the
dynamic feel of the pursuit itself. He passes through his successive
experiences like a wave-movement through water. For the older
Goethe the very notion of stasis dissolves into movement:
'Zustand ist ein albernes Wort; weil nichts steht und alles
beweglich ist' (to Niebuhr, 23 November 1812).

This is deeply disturbing to common assumptions. Men have
always been aware of movement and change, but as a threat to
what they valued, not as part of it. The ideal was something stable;

happiness was a condition to be sought after, secured, possessed and enjoyed. Movement and turbulence could and often did destroy it. The world could not be relied on. Hence a number of stock responses: in literature, the obsession with 'mutability', either in the form of the injunction 'carpe diem' (make the most of it while you can); or of elegy (lamenting its loss); or of pastoral idyll (wistfully pretend it once existed unimperilled in a golden age). And in philosophy: the idealism of Plato and after (aspire to know the absolutes beyond the mere world of sense). And in religion: renunciation (don't get too attached to what won't last, lay up treasure in heaven instead). All these responses, especially the attempts to link man with a changeless alternative world, have as their premiss the belief that anything subject to change cannot be real, or true, or satisfying in the long run. Change itself was the worm in the earthly apple.

Goethe questions this premiss, and by taking over change into his conception, not just of the world, but of happiness as man can attain it *in* the world, he implicitly questions much of Western thought. We can imagine him in dialogue with the great negators. With Schopenhauer, for instance, who triumphantly points out that even the fulfilment of desire is an illusory happiness, because desire will renew itself again, as sharp as before. To which Goethe replies: but that is what one would expect; it is the way man is; a creature of sequence, of fluctuation, changing in and with a world of flux, not a timeless being that could ever hope to reach a once-for-all goal. So Schopenhauer's desired nirvana is not a goal for such a creature; it is a non-goal that does not satisfy him but merely abolishes his very concept. Or with Pascal, who claims that all men's activities are so many diversions by which they evade the knowledge of their true being, its dependence on God and need for salvation; if only they realized that it is not each trivial goal that they are really pursuing, but the numbing distraction of the pursuit itself. To which Goethe replies: but of course the pursuit is more valuable than the goal; we are defined by movement; there is no still centre where man sits in a room and simply 'is' himself; there is no 'tabula rasa' lacking all inscription of activity that we could offer to God as man's absolute state.

In this grand debate, Goethe's only visible ally is Montaigne, who first dissolves man into a flux more extreme and more minutely and brilliantly observed than any previous student of mutability, and then gradually faces this human condition with a rich autumnal acceptance that equals Goethe's in conviction and at times in sheer beauty of expression:

> C'est une des principales obligations que j'aye à ma fortune, que le cours de mon estat corporel ayt esté conduit chasque chose en sa saison. J'en ay veu l'herbe et les fleurs et le fruit; et en vois la secheresse. Heureusement, puisque c'est naturellement.   (*Du repentir*)

Goethe does not say that our being and our happiness *should* not be static — he is not in that way a moralist; he says that they *cannot* be static, given our nature as the creatures we observably are in the observable world we inhabit. It is as fundamental a statement about the limitations of human nature as Kant's was about the limitations of human mind. Man can no more have absolute being than he can have absolute knowledge; he is linked into the world through his specific and inescapable constitution. But this is a statement of *acceptance* (as indeed Kant's was) not of lament:

> Lass den Anfang mit dem Ende
> Sich in *eins* zusammenziehn!
> Schneller als die Gegenstände
> Selber dich vorüberfliehn.
>
> ('Dauer im Wechsel'; HA, I, 247)

There may of course be a sense of pattern and achievement even in flux — 'Der Gehalt in deinem Busen/ Und die Form in deinem Geist' — just as there was for Montaigne 'une forme sienne, une forme maîtresse'.[3] Continuity may seem possible and desirable. So that to the question 'Sage, wie lebst du?' the answer can be given: 'ich lebe! Und wären hundert und hundert/ Jahre dem Menschen gegönnt, wünscht' ich mir morgen wie heut' (*Venezianische Epigramme* 92; HA, I, 182). There can be moments when the flux of things is concentrated into a particular significance by means of symbol. Faust can attain a single 'höchsten Augenblick' because it is one that has for its content an expectation of activity renewing itself without end. Movement is reconciled with the stasis of contemplation. Or, in the lyrical contemplation of the universe, a state of rest can be evoked which is the persisting pattern into which moving forces are shaped by inherent laws: 'Und alles

Drängen, alles Ringen/Ist ewige Ruh in Gott dem Herrn' (HA, I, 367). In the late philosophical poems a harmonious macrocosm matches the harmony of its poetic creator in a kind of cosmic idyll. And for Goethe it was even possible to imagine, in a grand conceit that replaces all other-worldly teleologies by a humanist one, a single supreme moment when the universe reaches its culmination, and cries out in pleasure at doing so. It is the moment when all its sublime mechanisms have produced human happiness:

> Denn wozu dient alle der Aufwand von Sonnen und Planeten und Monden, von Sternen und Milchstrassen, von Kometen und Nebelflecken, von gewordenen und werdenden Welten, wenn sich nicht zuletzt ein glücklicher Mensch unbewusst seines Daseins erfreut?
>
> (*Winckelmann*; HA, XII, 98)

It is not hard to think of one man who could be cast in that role.

What is the value and significance of all this? Why should Goethe's happiness concern us? Most obviously, because it offers a grand literary spectacle. In his most serene and vigorous writing — in the poems, the letters, in *Faust* — we can watch a scene or an experience being encountered, enjoyed, understood and interacted with in all its immediate richness and its underlying order by a sensibility of the greatest power yet also of the greatest delicacy. If we speak of poetic 'success', we mean something that goes far beyond the technicalities of aesthetic representation and touches on norms of feeling and being. The sense that we are seeing things as they should be seen runs counter to our customary belief in artistic pluralism; yet it is a sense that Goethe recreates every time we read him.

That is already a great boon; and it makes one want to say what Nietzsche said of Montaigne, who gives us a similar sense: 'Dass ein solcher Mensch geschrieben hat, dadurch ist wahrlich die Lust auf dieser Erde zu leben vermehrt worden'. And he goes on: 'Mit ihm würde ich es halten, wenn die Aufgabe gestellt wäre, es sich auf der Erde heimisch zu machen'.[4] Since the task inescapably *is* set us, Goethe's support is welcome; the more so since his life and work are so clearly opposed to certain modern received ideas. He stands for — he virtually is by himself — a positive culture; he affirms the structures of experience as they arise from the given nature of the world and of man; he is canonical in happiness. All this not as some kind of establishment plot to hide the real truth, but as the product of a tireless independent probing of life which begins with the revolution of the early writing and then broadens steadily into science, history, philosophy. From first to last, it is an individual vision; in other words, it satisfies the central criterion of modern culture, it is authentic. But —somewhat unusually — it is an authentic vision that finds or creates its own benign order. Subsequent revolutions in art have not done this. They too have claimed validity, as the expression of authentically individual thought and feeling. But they have not been canonical in happiness; they have been canonical in unhappiness and rejection of human experience. They dominate, at least in retrospect, the nineteenth century; and they dominate even more plainly and self-consciously the literature of the twentieth.

The reasons for this shift are all too familiar —'Weltschmerz', 'Angst', 'disinheritance'. But there are perhaps other reasons smaller in scale, and closer to the processes by which literature is actually created. And these may help us to understand how the larger factors work.

One is the idea that happiness is trivial and suffering profound. In a letter of 12 March 1806 to Friedrich de la Motte Fouqué, August Wilhelm Schlegel writes that Romantic poetry is 'inniger und geheimnisvoller als die klassische . . . weil die Griechen nur die Poetik der Freude ersonnen hatten'. It is not clear where he has mislaid Greek tragedy. Anyway, he goes on: 'Der Schmerz ist aber poetischer als das Vergnügen, und der Ernst als der Leichtsinn'; and he dismisses a poetry of 'schönes und freies Spiel' — a Goethean poetry, that is — in favour of a poetry of religious inspiration. This is part of the general drift towards what Goethe later, in conversation with Eckermann on 24 September 1827, called 'Lazarettpoesie', with its concentration on the 'Leiden und Jammer der Erde' and with 'Freude' offered only in the afterlife.

The new men's scorning of classical affirmation is partly explicable (like so much in early Romanticism) by the tactical needs of competing with the Classical achievement; and that may lead us on to ask whether another, deeper factor may not be the technical difference between writing affirmative poetry and writing the poetry of pain. Suffering may be 'more poetic' in the sense that it lends itself more readily to poetic formulation: it is easier to write poetry about. I said earlier that Goethe's poems of happiness 'stated the obvious'; but stating the obvious isn't easy. Goethe's directness only gives the *illusion* of ease. It is in fact an artistic technique — however instinctively used — of the first order. It cannot have been easy to see things clearly through the haze of past conventions; or to render happiness (which is essentially undramatic) without allowing it to seem flat, insipid, complacent. It was a delicate matter to see what it consisted in; to pick out the eloquent details from the pervading emotion; to join them in a persuasive pattern. Pain, by contrast, compels the attention unmistakably: it leaves no doubt of its location; it is potentially dramatic; it presses for utterance of an obvious kind —obvious in a quite different sense from the immediacy of happiness. Yet that is no index of its greater frequency or greater importance in human life; or of its greater claim to the poet's attention. Indeed, if the lineaments of pain are traced and the lineaments of happiness are not, an unbalanced picture will result.

Goethe himself makes essentially these points long before the slippery slope of Romanticism begins, in a letter to Lavater, his old friend and adversary. Lavater was one of those Christian negators of earthly happiness with whom Goethe had a prolonged dialogue; and as part of it in 1782 he sent Goethe a confession of his beliefs. The letter isn't preserved; but it must have been strongly self-analytical, and not very happy in tenor. For in a letter of 4 October 1782 Goethe replies that to get a true picture, a 'wahres Facit', out of such a document, the reader must make good its imbalance by what he calls an 'eigene psychologische Rechnungsoperation':

> Das, was der Mensch an sich bemerkt und fühlt, scheint mir der geringste Teil seines Daseyns. Es fällt ihm mehr auf was ihm fehlt, als das was er besitzt, er bemerkt mehr was ihn ängstiget, als das was ihn ergötzt und seine Seele erweitert; denn in allen angenehmen und guten Zuständen verliert die Seele das Bewusstseyn ihrer Selbst, wie der Körper auch, und wird nur durch unangenehme Empfindungen wieder an sich erinnert; und so wird meistentheils, der über sich selbst und seinen vergangenen

Zustand schreibt, das enge und schmerzliche aufzeichnen,
dadurch denn eine Person, wenn ich so sagen darf,
zusammenschrumpft.

Goethe's aperçu points up his own achievement in managing to
record his positive perceptions and happy emotions. But, more
generally: is it an exaggeration to say that the picture of human
experience since Goethe has suffered precisely from that
'Zusammenschrumpfen'? And is it possible that 'das enge und
schmerzliche' and 'was uns ängstiget' has become so much more
obtrusive, not just because life has got grimmer (who can really
say whether it has?) or because of the psychological and technical
difficulties of perceiving and rendering the 'angenehmen und
guten Zustände' which would restore the shrunken picture to full
life size?

Sometimes this technical difficulty is stated in a text. In *The Mill
on the Floss* (VI, 3) George Eliot says that a heroine's life with 'few
vicissitudes . . . hardly has been written; for the happiest women,
like the happiest nations, have no history'. André Gide's narrator
in *L'Immoraliste* says: 'Les plus belles oeuvres des hommes sont
obstinément douloureuses. Que serait le récit du bonheur? Rien
que ce qui le prépare, puis ce qui le détruit, ne se raconte.' Even
Tolstoy opens *Anna Karenina* with the idea that all happy families
are alike, but every unhappy family is unhappy in its own way
('even', because few writers, in the event, have rendered happiness
as splendidly as Tolstoy does). Or again, the technical difficulty
may be implicit in a writer's failure to convey a positive vision to
which he is in some sense committed: Heine's failure in his
middle years to act out or recreate convincingly a Goethean
sensual harmony; Kafka's failure to express in his fiction the
positive conceptions for which he could find mystical terms in his
diary aphorisms. Even such a great celebrator of life as Walt
Whitman partially fails for lack of the formal control and
concentration that would give the gesture of acceptance real
poetic density.

But however the difficulty appears, one thing we cannot expect:
and that is that readers, singly and as cultural public, will easily
perform the 'eigene psychologische Rechnungsoperation', and
balance out for themselves the images of anxiety or radical
rejection which disturb the proportions of the picture that
literature offers of life. So that if happiness is not represented,

difficult as it is for us to focus and preserve our own experience of it as it slips away, it will go by default and be abandoned to sentimental 'Trivialliteratur'. That will then mark it down as inherently trivial. What is, at least in part, a *literary* failure leaves the way open for sweeping *existential* assumptions. The result is a culture in which pessimistic writing generates a pessimistic climate, which in turn makes pessimistic writing seem the only possibility.[5]

I am getting on to dangerous ground. Arguments in favour of 'positive' culture and a literature of acceptance often go hand in hand with social and political conservatism. In the German tradition they go with the ideologically suspect notion of 'timeless' art: 'Dichtung', rather than 'Literatur', which is elevated above real life and able to go on contemplating and creating beauty, whatever is going on down below. Appeals to cultural 'health' against alleged 'decadence' have a nasty political history. Even outside the German tradition, the idea of affirmation may at first sight be worrying to the liberal mind: 'The imagination of felicity', writes Lionel Trilling in *Beyond Culture* (Peregrine Books, 1967), 'is difficult for us to exercise. We feel that it is a betrayal of our awareness of our world of pain, that it is politically inappropriate.' But are we right to feel that? Trilling goes on to quote precisely Schiller's account of idyll; and he suggests that for Schiller the representation of happiness is 'virtually the poet's political duty' (p. 67f.).

This is a surprise. We don't expect to find something as bland as happiness on the progressive side. The usual assumption is that progressive social attitudes go hand in hand with the modern or (in Trilling's term) 'adversary' culture, just as surely as conservatism is linked with 'affirmation'. The adversary culture criticizes, rejects and aims to destroy what it sees as 'specious good', which of course includes the fixed values of philistine bourgeois society (p. 78). But it also rejects the more basic, non-social phenomena of pleasure, beauty, benevolent nature and harmonious experience; certainly, none of them are prominent as a help or consolation to man in works of the dark modern canon. Yet in rejecting these things too, and accepting as a norm the gloom that is left, modern culture deprives itself of so many allies in the practical tasks which its account of the world shows are urgent. Nature was an ally to Schiller, to Hölderlin — even to Brecht. Now, the sense of a benevolent order is missing from major literature and fashionable philosophy; it can only be found among ethologists, ecologists and natural scientists.[6] So Trilling is forced to conclude not just that radical modernism, when sanctified by syllabus, yielded a set of glib pessimistic clichés (which is bad enough); but that these clichés, and perhaps even the legitimate reception of modern works, are impoverishing and disabling:

> The modern self-pity is certainly not without its justifi-
> cation; but, if the circumstances that engender it are ever
> to be overcome, we must wonder whether this work can
> be done by minds which are taught in youth to accept
> these sad conditions of ours as the only right objects of
> contemplation. (p. 21).

In other words, we need a conception of happiness, and not just of misery, as the mainspring of our social activity. The richer and fuller and more challenging our conception of happiness, the better our politics will be. For the Enlightenment, pity was the prime social virtue that literature should foster. But pity alone isn't enough; and certainly not when it has largely turned into self-pity.

Trilling's argument (pp. 62ff.) cries out for a positive figure as contrast and antidote. But it harks back to nothing more embracing than Keats's and Wordsworth's notion of 'pleasure'. Goethe he occasionally mentions but seems substantially unaware of; yet his need for an alternative to modern negativity which is not a mere 'idiot literature' (p. 80) could be met by Goethe and those Goethean qualities I have been trying to remind you of.

The question then is: What effect could Goethe possibly have? How ready is contemporary culture to be corrected by the past, or even to engage in dialogue with it? At best it seems uncertain how live a force Goethe is in German culture today. The present celebrations prove nothing. They were inevitable as part of the continuity which it is the job of public institutions and cultural diplomacy to maintain. Such flurries of historical piety may amount to no more than the putting on display of a historical curiosity. It is not long since some of Goethe's home critics were agreeing that he wasn't read, not even by themselves, not even before they sat down to dismiss him.[7] The self-parody of this admission, the realization that this couldn't be *quite* right, was perhaps a hopeful sign. Still it may seem quaint to set this hundred-and-fifty-year-old success story against the assertion that goes on being unquestioningly pushed at us — as in a headline in the feuilleton section of a recent number of *Die Zeit* (31 July 1981): 'Die zeitgenössische Literatur ist eine Angst-literatur'. The literary outlook seems set as 'continuing overcast'.

We can of course argue that even when there is a great deal to be genuinely anxious about — indeed, precisely then — it is defeatist to ignore any possible sources of hope and vigour. Darkness will get darker if we do nothing to lighten it. But there are well-known obstacles before Goethe can be drawn on trustingly by his own culture. They are partly grounded in German history, for whose sins he like other writers has had to serve as a whipping-boy. He is still tarred with the brush of his grotesque nineteenth-century reception, which read his conception of 'Ordnung' as an ideal of social conformism. He is still suspect for having been a court employee, even though he was never associated with a centre of major power, never had any broad political influence, was a compassionate and unusually efficient administrator, held as critical a view of feudalism as he did of revolution, and was always a half-detached, ironic, Jacques-like figure in his relations with the Weimar Court, sometimes satiric, sometimes (as when he ran away to Italy) positively anarchic. He only ever accepted the natural universe with any enthusiasm, not the social and political world. At most he thought the status quo a somewhat safer bet than the uncertain consequences — after 1793, the almost certain unpleasant consequences — of revolution. Even his undeniable conservative tendencies in old age, which made him less liberal than his master Karl August, are no reason to disqualify the persisting dynamism of his work, in which movement and change and the human need for change are as central as ever. The conservatism was a feature of the empirical person; to let it obscure from view what the intelligible person wrote is to practise a simplistically destructive form of biographism.

In other words, the obstacles that stand between Goethe and the German public are at root bad reading habits: a failure or refusal to identify literature as a distinctive mode of being and acting which can provide vital impulses for everyday; a failure to abstract and transfer. Even his famous self-fulfilment as the works record it need not be envied and resented and decried in contrast with the tragic fate of other writers. Even this can be valued for its representativity, as an embodiment of what man as such can be. We have to say of it what he said of his time in Italy — it wasn't just his personal pleasure. He might have said with Lynkeus der Türmer, whose sharp eyes also found the world acceptable: 'Nicht allein mich zu ergetzen,/Bin ich hier so hoch gestellt' (*Faust*, lines 11304f.). Goethe's happiness, as I began by suggesting, was his historical mission.

Finally, where does he figure in our activity? Still as an element in the syllabus, no doubt. But perhaps no longer compulsory, having to compete instead with the more recently canonized. Well, he can do that. Given the deadening effect his late nineteenth-century institutionalization had, we would not want to make him an *official* norm: an establishment alternative to the 'adversary' and 'subversive' authenticity of Büchner, Kleist and Kafka, or a base from which to snipe at their and other writers' darker view.

But if we avoid that, we can also avoid implying through the seeming authority of the syllabus, and the way we teach it, that those authors are the *new* norm: necessarily more profound and truer in their grasp of human experience than this old survival from a prelapsarian age of easy contentment. The picture can be kept balanced by including in it Goethe's authentic vision too. His authenticity is the equal of any. And paradoxically he has his own subversiveness still, of the most permanently valuable kind: his example of happiness can at any time challenge a world that never was and never will be shaped to yield happiness easily.

Notes to Goethe and Happiness

1. Quoting *Ethics,* Pt. II, prop. xl, note II — not, pace HA, Briefe I, 758, Pt. V, prop. xxv, Proof, where a similar wording occurs but without the phrase 'essentiae formalis'.

2. For clarification of concepts of happiness, see Elizabeth Telfer, *Happiness,* New Studies in Practical Philosophy (London, 1980).

3.   *Du repentir*. Montaigne's other image of relative stability is 'estre chez moy' — a striking similarity to Goethe's 'das Wohnen in sich selbst'.

4.   *Unzeitgemässe Betrachtungen* III, *Schopenhauer als Erzieher*, 2.

5.   There has been sporadic critical protest about this state of affairs. See, for instance, Hans Egon Holthusen, 'Über den sauren Kitsch', in Holthusen, *Ja und Nein* (Munich, 1954); or Emil Staiger, 'Literatur und Öffentlichkeit', the speech which set going the 'Zürcher Literaturstreit' of 1966-67. The whole controversy is documented in *Sprache im technischen Zeitalter*, 22 (1967) and 26 (1968).

6.   For a philosophical sifting and constructive development of recent work in ethology see Mary Midgley's *Beast and Man* (Hassocks, 1978). Even the most extreme attempt of pure natural science to reduce the universe to its simplest principles concludes that 'the universe has come awake during . . . the epoch of benevolence' as P.W. Atkins says in *The Creation* (Oxford and San Francisco, 1981), p. 125.

7.   *Literaturmagazin 2: Von Goethe lernen?* (Reinbek, 1974), pp. 28, 49f.

The Metaphor of Silence   Victor Lange

I

It's not surprising that in a century as deeply committed as the eighteenth to articulating its convictions — to discourse and explication in language, and to all the rhetorical strategies of speech — writers should return again and again to the haunting experience of linguistic insufficiency: from that 'ambiguity in words', as Locke put it, to the line that marks the limits of a describable or communicable universe. Since speech and writing remained the central preoccupation of that critical age, their elucidating capacity was denied not only in argument but in the demonstrative assertion of the efficacy of silence: inferior in its discursive scope, but forceful in its challenge to any unexamined trust in conventional modes of speech.

To the metaphor, or symbolism, of silence writers seem to have turned with an awareness, not just of the inadequacy of language, but also of those mythical or ritualistic gestures that suggest a reality of experience beyond the uttered, maybe always unutterable: the ineffable word. This double impulse of faith in language, on the one hand, doubt in its ability to convey the full energy of reflection or intuition, on the other, is the tenor of all linguistic inquiry during the Age of Enlightenment. From Còndillac, Süssmilch, Hamann and Herder to the Romantic poets, a Novalis or a Hölderlin, the sanctions for the truth of speech, for the validity of its signs, were sought in reason as well as inspiration, in religious prophecy as in secular convictions.

If language was accepted as an indispensable instrument of civilized social traffic, it was also in constant danger of being devalued and debased by those who used it irresponsibly. Hence the failure of language, its use and abuse were common topics of stage and fiction: the comedies of Congreve, Sheridan and Fielding cultivate laughable offenders against the conventions of speech; the novels from Richardson, Fielding and Sterne to H. Mackenzie confirm or persiflage in their heroes and heroines a stereotypical recourse to silence at moments of surprise whether in pleasure or offense. Discussions of the rhetoric of acting, of Garrick's extravagant histrionic distortions of a given text, no less than Diderot's disquisitions on the speech of the deaf and the dumb, led to such systematic accounting of telling gestures beyond speech as J.J. Engel's *Mimik*, an elaborate grammar of communicative signals, in which silence was urged as a device of special effectiveness.

These indications of the limited range of speech or, concomitantly, of a potential of meaning beyond language, become part of the aesthetic vocabulary of the late eighteenth century. In the figure of the hermit, who demonstratively rejects the convivial uses of speech, this experience was frequently made plausible. The solitary, whether in serious or trivial literature, is one who has chosen to live apart from his fellow men, often inaccessible in a landscape of forbidding forests and mountains. Whatever the reasons for his withdrawal — religious or secular, wilful or devout, disappointed in ambition or love — he is resolved not to be distracted by an inane society from pursuing his vision in silence. He imitates the venerable hermits of the great religions, imposing upon himself something of the arcane discipline of early Christians, of the ancient mysteries, of those who abstained from speech as a means of meditation with the ultimate aim of expressing reverence before the Un-sayable. The solitary may, in the spirit of Rousseau, have sought refuge from a debilitating civilization; but he did not need to spend his days in total abstinence from the advantages of the world he had left. Indeed, in *Erscheinungen am See Oneida*, a novel by Sophie LaRoche, a curious traveller finds him comfortably installed on an almost inaccessible island; sustained in his austere life by the works of poets and philosophers, who strengthen his determination to engage in silent meditation rather than unprofitable talk with the foolish in the world beyond his retreat.

In German literature, the chain of such figures seems to remain unbroken well beyond their medieval or Baroque representation. It recurs in humanist and popular writing wherever the mystical experience is to be rendered in its radical form, unmediated by human speech. In the sceptical intellectual climate of the eighteenth and early nineteenth centuries, the solitary takes on an increasingly secular cast; and the silence which continues to constitute his central characteristic is now rationalized in a variety of impulses and projected in a multitude of gestures of reticence — awed; defiant, touching or, as in several of E.T.A. Hoffmann's characters, even ambiguous to the point of seeming insanity.

The silent hermit is the object of ridicule in Lessing's early verse-tale *Der Eremit*; he is the counter-figure to the exuberant seducer Satyros in Goethe's brief drama of that name, and the disdainful recluse in Lenz's *Die Kleinen*. One of the characters in Klinger's play *Sturm und Drang* withdraws into a cave to protect in silence his sense of natural integrity from a despised society; Al Hafi and the 'Klosterbrüder' in *Nathan* have known the silent and withdrawn life. Goethe's Erwin plays at being a hermit to soothe the pain of having been rejected by Elinore; in Lenz's *Waldbruder* the sentimental lover Herz becomes a solitary to cultivate his love for the countess in defiance of an unfeeling society; and Werdo Senne, the hermit who persuades Brentano's Godwi to withdraw into his refuge, plays his harp and sings in melancholy parallel to Mignon's father in Goethe's *Wilhelm Meister*, unwilling to speak and possessing the remarkable power to seal the lips of others. Alfonso, the hermit in Wieland's *Oberon*, protects the integrity of his poetry by silently appealing to the all-encompassing spirit of Nature; and for Novalis's Friedrich von Hohenzollern the sublime experience of historical continuity illuminates and silences the restless mind. There are few works either of trivial or sophisticated fiction in late eighteenth-century German literature in which a refugee from private sorrow, or a more general despair at the obtuseness of heart or spirit, is not introduced as a reminder of the strength of silent inwardness over any enlightened faith in discourse; of the difficulties in articulating complexity in language; of the failure of public speech to convey and resolve private concerns.

Yet, as the solitary becomes a favourite stereotype he ceases to serve as an adequate metaphor for conveying the subtler and more complex tensions between speech and silence. Indeed, no

single figure seems able to represent fully the ever more serious
implications of the problematical uncertainties of language. The
failure of expression, of communication, of intimating the
implications of feelings and ideas, begins to assume thematic
dimensions. It is rendered with relentless logic in Laurence
Sterne's *Tristram Shandy*, disguising its seriousness in scenes,
moments and passages of oblique humour and irony. Sterne's
craft of articulation — whether through suspending a sentence or
withholding responses to it — creates a sustained narrative in
which multivalence and ambiguity of communication become
the very topic of the telling. The subtlety of his perception of the
mobility and strategic deviousness of speech remains unsurpassed.

II

It is in such a context that the statement that Goethe was, early and
late, committed to *language* really comes into its own. Committed
to it as the medium — preferable to the figurative arts — that
could describe and reflect whatever he wanted to say, whether as
poet, scientist or correspondent. Speech was, throughout his life,
part of that cosmos of natural resources by which the human
being defines and constitutes itself. His early letters are evidence
of an astonishing exuberance of imaginative speech which was
personal to him, even though it may have been from Herder that
he had learned the use of forceful *Klangworte* or *Machtworte* as
vehicles of inspired poetic speech.

Yet he was soon to feel, in the course of his work as a reviewer
for the *Frankfurter gelehrte Anzeigen*, that even the prophetic energy
of inspired speech could not of itself assure an adequate reception
in his audience. And in a piece entitled 'Nachrede statt der
versprochenen Vorrede' on 29 December 1772 he recognized
unhappily that 'trying to communicate with the public could only
result in misunderstandings etc. etc.'. In a more dithyrambic
piece on 'speaking in tongues' a year later he argued that the
incommensurable presence of the spirit has ceased to be perceived:
'In der Einschränkung unsrer Menschlichkeit ist nicht mehr als
eine Ahndung davon zu tappen'. His desire to give testimony to
the spirit in his own poetic speech — 'Vom Geist erfüllt, in der
Sprache des Geists, des Geists Geheimnisse verkündigen' — is all

too often paralysed by his doubt in the reliability of the uttered word (GA, IV, 146). This, of course, is the key to the theme of 'the word inadequate to the logos' which haunts Faust. The intricate sign-character of language; its uncertain capacity to correlate intention and reception; the felt distance between affirmation and doubt, pronouncement and silence — these are the topics to which the young Goethe returns over and over again in his letters, his poetry and his critical reflections. Without their constant urgency, and without the example of similar preoccupations in contemporary fiction — especially Sterne's masterly use of indirection in speech — a novel such as *Werther* could hardly have been conceived, let alone written.

As that passionately self-centred character moves from eagerly experienced sociability to the solitude of isolation and despair, we are made aware of the chief sympton of his disintegration: his loss of the power to articulate a disjointed state of mind. This youthful novel, composed with an astonishing sense of the line between the efficacy as well as the limitations of narrative conventions, of speech ebbing inexorably into silence, is the record, transposed into fiction, of Goethe's own perception of the tantalizing ambiguity of words, and of his resolve to provide metaphorical configurations that might counter obtuseness and misunderstanding.

The metaphor of silence is henceforth offered, throughout Goethe's works and correspondence, not merely as the ready coin of stylized privacy, but as a confession of the discrepancy between feelings and the words available to indicate their subtlety as well as their strength. The sentiment echoed in Faust's plea to Gretchen he also offers in his own letters to Auguste von Stolberg: 'Lass mein Schweigen dir sagen, was keine Worte sagen können', or again: 'Könntest du mein Schweigen verstehen! Liebes Gustgen! Ich kann, ich kann nichts sagen!' (14-19 September 1775 and 11 February 1776). To his friend Kestner he writes on 28 September 1777: 'nicht dass ich euch vergessen habe, sondern dass ich im Zustande des Schweigens bin . . .'. And in his letters to Charlotte von Stein he speaks repeatedly of that sense of life and bliss that is beyond expression: 'In uns ist Leben und — ich weiss wohl was ich will aber wie sagen?' (13-16 September 1777); or again on 9 January 1779: 'Einen guten Morgen von Ihrem stummen Nachbar. Das Schweigen ist so schön dass ich wünschte es Jahre lang halten zu dürfen.' Against Lavater's religious exclamations, he defends, on 9 August 1782, his own reverent silence: 'ich bin still und verschweige was mir Gott und die Natur offenbart'. This insufficiency of speech he feels acutely as he confronts objects or topics of some emotional consequence. 'Alles Reden und Beschreiben hilft bei sinnlichen, ja auch bei moralischen Gegen- ständen nichts', he insists to Charlotte von Stein on 2 December 1786. However exuberant his letters, when he is with her he seems often enough to have withdrawn into silence; so that she is reported to have said of him in a conversation on 31 January 1786 '[er] sei der immer Schweigende' (GA, XXII, 150). A term which carries the specific meaning of suspended speech, and in Goethe's later work assumes an almost emblematic function, first occurs with emphasis in a letter to Plessing of 26 July 1782: 'mitten im Glück [lebe ich] in einem anhaltenden Entsagen'.

These confessions — half impassioned, half sentimental — of resignation in silence contribute something like the ground bass of his letters before his journey to Italy. In Italy and afterwards the tone and the focus of his reflections on the efficacy of language change noticeably. What he now deplores is not the subjective failure of speech, the discrepancy between intention and utterance, but the limited comprehension or congeniality of his audience. The gap that exists between the proffered signs of intellectual or emotional engagement and the conscious or unconscious resis- tance in the listener to an appropriate, or at least discreet, readiness to share in the opportunities of dialogue or discourse:

> Reden schwanken so leicht herüber hinüber, wenn viele
> Sprechen und jeder nur sich im eigenen Worte, sogar
> auch
> Nur sich selbst im Worte vernimmt, das der andere sagte.
> (*Episteln* I)

The growing importance of convention; the careful use of speech as information or persuasion rather than personal monologue; language as the instrument of social traffic, guarded, or even deliberately withheld; silence rather than attempted sharing — all of this seems now an important element in his relationship to others. The modest equipment of his German readers increasingly suggests caution in offering too much: '. . . es ist Pflicht andern nur dasjenige zu sagen, was sie aufnehmen können' (*Wilhelm*

Meisters Wanderjahre, 1, 3). In a poem of his *Divan* he puts the same thought less ponderously:

> Das glücklichste Wort, es wird verhöhnt,
> Wenn der Hörer ein Schiefohr ist.
>
> ('Buch der Betrachtungen', 1)

We know, of course, that he made it a point to keep his affairs to himself. 'Ich habe mir zum Gesetz gemacht', he wrote to Jenny von Voigts on 21 June 1781, 'über mich selbst und das Meinige ein gewissenhaftes Stillschweigen zu beobachten'. And while he seems eager to read from his own work in progress, he is careful not to elaborate on his literary projects: careful to mystify rather than inform the curious; to mask rather than reveal his intentions. 'Denn eigentlich soll man nicht reden von dem, was man tun will', he would write to Boisserée on 22 October 1826; 'nicht von dem, was man tut, noch was man getan hat'. In other words he remained resolved to keep personal matters to himself. As for instance in one of his posthumous reflections on the differing modes of language in all spheres of thought: 'Ich weiss recht gut woher und wohin, warum und wozu, erkläre mich aber weiter nicht darüber' (GA, IX, 614).[1] Reticence and silence were his defences against dissipating his energies in premature or un-rewarding discourse; one of the results of a conviction that the intricacies of thought or feeling are all too easily trivialized by presumptuous questioners. One highly entertaining demon-stration of this conviction is the burlesque disputation between Mephistopheles and the student. Faust's despair when faced with the limits of knowledge is tantamount to the experience of incommunicable insight. 'Das Beste, was du wissen kannst, / Darfst du den Buben doch nicht sagen' is Mephisto's common-sense echo of Faust's state of mind. And it is the obverse of this conclusion that Mephistopheles should encourage the student to learn to manipulate his listeners by using speech as shrewdly as possible: to numb and confuse as well as to conceal his own ignorance.

> Viel Denken, mehr Empfinden
> Und wenig Reden . . .

he suggests in the *Zahme Xenien*, as if in anticipation of that much quoted utterance by Montan in *Wilhelm Meisters Wanderjahre* (II, 9):

> . . . das Liebste, und das sind doch unsre Überzeugungen,
> muss jeder im tiefsten Ernst bei sich selbst bewahren,
> jeder weiss nur für sich was er weiss und das muss er
> geheim halten; wie er es ausspricht, sogleich ist der
> Widerspruch rege . . . Wenn man einmal weiss, worauf
> alles ankommt, hört man auf gesprächig zu sein . . .
> Denken und Tun, Tun und Denken, das ist die Summe
> aller Weisheit.

Silence, Goethe declares in a more solemn key in his *Natürliche Tochter* (1, 3), is the premise of all strategic designs:

> Gar vieles kann, gar vieles muss geschehn,
> Was man mit Worten nicht bekennen darf.

Or again, in this same unfinished work (1, 5):

> Geheimnis nur verbürget unsre Taten;
> Ein Vorsatz, mitgeteilt, ist nicht mehr dein;
> Der Zufall spielt mit deinem Willen schon.

In these and other statements we feel something of Goethe's belief in the ritualistic effectiveness of silence. He summed it up in his *Tag- und Jahreshefte* for 1803:

> Einen sehr tiefen Sinn hat jener Wahn, dass man, um
> einen Schatz wirklich zu heben und zu ergreifen,
> stillschweigend verfahren müsse, kein Wort sprechen
> dürfe, wie viel Schreckliches und Ergötzendes auch von
> allen Seiten erscheinen möge.

The characteristic formula in which Goethe reiterates the wisdom of not making universal experiences or propositions explicit is the phrase 'öffentliches/offenbares Geheimnis'. 'Es gibt', he notes in a letter to one of the most interesting of his correspondents, Ch. L. Friedrich Schultz, on 28 November 1821, with explicit emphasis upon the linguistic implications of that phrase, 'so viele offenbare Geheimnisse, weil das Gefühl derselben bei wenigen ins Bewusstsein tritt und diese denn, weil sie sich und andere zu beschädigen fürchten, eine innere Aufklärung nicht zum Worte kommen lassen.' To the question, 'Welches ist das wichtigste Geheimnis?' the 'Golden King' of Goethe's *Märchen* replies: 'Das offenbare'. This 'open secret' should be given voice, and understood; much as silence, with its own resonance and demands, should be heard and shared.

The aura of mystery which the notion of an 'offenbares Geheimnis' intimated, ever since its first occurrence, as early as 1777, in the cryptic poem 'Harzreise im Winter', is almost automatically invoked whenever Goethe hopes to convey something of the infinitely challenging dimensions of natural phenomena.

> Geheimnisvoll am lichten Tag,
> Lässt sich Natur des Schleiers nicht berauben . . .

he had written in *Faust I* (lines 672f.). And 'das geheime Wirken und Walten der Natur' of which he would speak to Eckermann on 20 June 1831 — however difficult to render in plain discursive terms, but far from suggesting resignation in the face of hermetic inscrutability — is the standing formula that points to a double impulse in his scientific efforts. On the one hand, unceasing attempts at objectifying the structures of the natural world; on the other, an unchanging resolve not to underrate the immense difficulties of giving an adequate account of that effort.

> Betrachtet, forscht, die Einzelnheiten sammelt,
> Naturgeheimnis werde nachgestammelt,

he would write as a late precipitate of his scientific endeavour at the end of his 'Marienbad Elegy'. It is the wish to give coherent voice to this involved procedure that constantly provides him with the central topic of art. In one of his best known maxims, for example: 'Wem die Natur ihr offenbares Geheimnis zu enthüllen anfängt, der empfindet eine unwiderstehliche Sehnsucht nach ihrer würdigsten Auslegerin, der Kunst' (GA, IX, 518). With evident reference to this charge upon art and poetry Goethe remind us of the supreme achievement of the supreme poet, who takes the awesome function of the world-spirit upon himself:

> Shakespeare gesellt sich zum Weltgeist; er durchdringt die Welt wie jener; beiden ist nichts verborgen; aber wenn des Weltgeists Geschäft ist, Geheimnisse vor, ja oft nach der Tat zu bewahren, so ist es der Sinn des Dichters, das Geheimnis zu verschwätzen und uns vor, oder doch gewiss in der Tat zu Vertrauten zu machen . . . das Geheimnis muss heraus, und sollten es die Steine verkünden.   (*Shakespeare und kein Ende*, I)

In all these confessional statements Goethe presupposes the centrality of language for every form of communication. He was never plagued by doubts about 'die alten ewigen Naturmaximen, wornach der Mensch dem Menschen durch die Sprache verständlich wird' (to Zelter, 11 March 1832). Nevertheless, speaking and doing were, for him, by no means self-evidently joined. During a journey through Switzerland in 1797 he found himself reflecting '. . . dass der Mensch die Rede eigentlich für die höchste Handlung hält, so wie man vieles tun darf, was man nicht sagen soll'. This double impulse of affirmation and doubt in the adequacy of speech will go on recurring throughout his life. -

> Da die Sprache das Organ gewesen, wodurch ich mich während meines Lebens am meisten und liebsten den Mitlebenden mitteilte, so musste ich darüber, besonders in spätern Zeiten, reflektieren . . . und so habe ich doch aufs deutlichste begreifen lernen, dass die Sprache nur ein Surrogat ist, wir mögen nun das was uns innerlich beschäftigt oder das was uns von aussen anregt ausdrücken wollen.
>
> (Letter to Ch. L. Friedrich Schultz, 11 March 1816)

It would, he thought, be better to remain forever silent than to contribute to the inescapable obfuscation of the traffic in words:

> . . . denn leider sind Worte dem Menschen gewöhnlich Surrogate, er denkt und weiss es meistenteils besser als er sich ausspricht. Der Redliche schweigt zuletzt, weil er nicht auch mit schlechter Spezerei ein schmutziges Gewerbe treiben mag.[2]

'Sensible speech' was for Goethe the precondition of communication. And recognition of the eminent importance of convention in the deployment of language produced that ceremonious and generalizing style of his late works and letters. Even in that manner, the difficulties of speaking unambiguously, and the appropriateness of remaining silent instead, are recurrent motifs. In his *Elective Affinities*, a novel which has as one of its more important themes the relationship between decorous speech and silence, he offers in a telling aphorism the conviction that no one would say much in the company of others if he knew how often he had misunderstood them. And there is an evident biographical core to one of the maxims incorporated in *Wilhelm Meisters Wanderjahre*: 'Ich schweige zu vielem still; denn ich mag die Menschen nicht irre machen' (GA, IX, 564). Speech and its failures appear as facets of the same linguistic consciousness: 'Sobald man spricht, beginnt man schon zu irren' (GA, I, 456). They are ingredients in the uncertain and intricate potential of articulation. He sums up his never-modified reservations in one of his last letters, the letter of 15 March 1832 to K.M. Sternberg: 'Die Sprache ist nicht auf alles eingerichtet, und wir wissen oft nicht recht, ob wir endlich sehen, schauen, denken, erinnern, phantasieren oder glauben' (WA, iv, XLIX, 271).

Yet it is not only a resigned acceptance of the limits of speech that produces silence. On the contrary; on a high level of social or existential sophistication, silence may well be the proud gesture of a state of mind, or a human relationship, beyond the narrow traffic of current language. It is the metaphor of civilized insight. 'Von der besten Gesellschaft sagte man', he suggests in 1826 in a series of statements that hinge upon his classicist faith in the energies of art and poetry, 'ihr Gespräch ist unterrichtend, ihr Schweigen bildend' (GA, IX, 538). We need only recall that magisterial plea 'Sagt es niemand, nur den Weisen, / Weil die Menge gleich verhöhnet' or Mignon's fervent injunction 'Heiss mich nicht reden, heiss mich schweigen', to recognize beyond the particular narrative context Goethe's solemn reminder, without metaphysical pathos, that there is nobility in withholding rather than disclosing a grave truth. If in one perspective Goethe can affirm the serene pleasure of speech — 'Was ist erquicklicher als Licht?' the King asks in *Das Märchen*, and the Serpent replies, 'Das Gespräch' — he can also insist, and with equal seriousness, upon the pre-eminent importance of reticence: 'Doch es ist ein altes Gesetz; ich schweig und verehre' (*Roman Elegies*, XIX).

This conjunction of an imperative of secretiveness and the promise of a state of shared insight; of perfect awareness of the sustaining organic order; of felt sympathy or respect, even reverence, for what may be claimed as privileged belief: this is the signature common to that singularly rich canon of metaphors of silence which — whether as 'Schweigen' or 'Verschwiegenheit', 'Verschweigen' or 'Verstummen', 'Geheimnis' or 'Ent-sagen', or extended into 'Rätsel, künstlich mit Worten verschränkt' — echo throughout Goethe's later works.

III

The sources of Goethe's metaphorical elaborations of silence are not difficult to find. One is the neo-Platonic ingredient of his thinking which prompts his confident belief in the symbolic mode: 'Man bedenkt niemals genug, dass eine Sprache eigentlich nur symbolisch, nur bildlich sei und die Gegenstände niemals unmittelbar, sondern nur im Widerscheine ausdrücke' (GA, XVI, 203). The 'act' of silence projects the object of reflection in an analogous manner. It is the oblique rendering of a specific communicative intention; a performance that is never, in Goethe's practice, a denial of sense, or of an ability to share in it, but the symbolic rejoinder to a challenge. It does not, as so often in the literature of our own day, interrupt, terminate or invalidate the relationship between communicating partners; but, on the contrary, maintains, even intensifies, that relationship in alert mutual attention. Even where silence is intended to assert the dignity of privacy over the public utterance of speech, it lays claims to be recognized as a demonstrative act.

Such an active and positive display of silence owes, on the other hand, much to those anthropological traditions in which silence suggests an exceptional degree of concentration as well as a state of mind that should be maintained at moments of intense contemplation. The ancient warning to refrain from speech during certain cult practices, the *favete linguis*, was — in a secularized spirit — revived as part of the freemasonic ritual. To such a symbolic or allegoric gesture Goethe turns frequently, so that the topic of silence emerges in innumerable fictional scenes and figures which give concreteness and resonance to the tenor of his more general reflections.

His belief in the efficacy of silence, in the need to protect evanescent experience from intrusion or profanation — persistently touched on in autobiographical documents — recurs throughout his poetry in pregnant metaphors and motifs. That fragment of a religious epic poem 'Die Geheimnisse' chooses a freemasonic key to touch upon the mystery of the Divine and its approximation in symbolic or emblematic signs. A masonic

poem of similar temper elaborates its title, 'Verschwiegenheit', in
a voice that recalls the bliss of secretiveness to which so many of
the *Divan* poems returned:

> Wenn die Liebste zum Erwidern
> Blick auf Liebesblicke beut,
> Singt ein Dichter gern in Liedern,
> Wie ein solches Glück erfreut!
> Aber Schweigen bringet Fülle
> Reicheren Vertrauns zurück;
> Leise, leise! Stille, stille!
> Das ist erst das wahre Glück.   (GA, I, 502)

One of the intellectual impulses that produced the longer of his
West-Eastern cycles was that 'Rätselhaft-Unauflösliche' he had
soon recognized as a particularly arresting feature of oriental
poetry (GA, III, 416). This phrase then serves him as a critical
precept appropriate to poems designed 'die wunderlich auf-
gegebenen Rätsel zu lösen' (GA, III, 478), and is subsequently
enlarged into a key formula that gives access to the subtle forms of
disguise which the *Divan* cycle offers in such profusion: 'Der
geistreiche Mensch . . . betrachtet alles, was sich den Sinnen
darbietet, als eine Vermummung, wohinter ein höheres geistiges
Leben sich schalkhaft-eigensinnig versteckt' (GA, III, 493). The
'Buch der Sprüche' contains 'laconic parables' in which human
situations are touched upon, 'ohne dass dabei ausgesprochen
werde, was gut oder bös sei' (GA, III, 502). Speech and silence —
'ein gesprochenes Wort' and 'was sich schweigend nur entfaltet!'
— these alternate throughout as 'cyphers' intimating and evoking
the abundance of a life of shared happiness. But it is in silence that
the moment of bliss is fully experienced:

> Was ich euch offenbaret
> War längst ein frommer Brauch,
> Und wenn ihr es gewahret,
> So schweigt und nutzt es auch.   ('Buch Suleika')

The very paradox of the poet's uttering the unsayable, his
constant recourse to the metaphor of 'ein öffentliches Geheimnis',
of secrecy turned into confession, is the gist of Hatem's most
profound stanza:

Dichten zwar ist Himmelsgabe,
Doch im Erdeleben Trug.

Erst sich im Geheimnis wiegen,
Dann verplaudern früh und spat!
Dichter ist umsonst verschwiegen,
Dichten selbst ist schon Verrat.   ('Das Schenkenbuch')

And it is in one of the poems that conclude the cycle, in the 'Buch des Paradieses', that speech beyond words leads to that contemplation of sublime love in which the *Divan* poems culminate:

Ton und Klang jedoch entwindet
Sich dem Worte selbstverständlich,
Und entschiedener empfindet
Der Verklärte sich unendlich . . .

Bis im Anschaun ewger Liebe
Wir verschweben, wir verschwinden.

The resonant mystery of greatness, and the silence appropriate to the poet's slowly evolving awareness of it, had also provided the variously shaded ground of the *Roman Elegies*. Though present in every encounter, it is fully unfolded as the theme of the twentieth. And projected as a gesture of infinitely touching surrender to the inexorable command of Hermes, who beckons the dead, silence is invoked in a most serene configuration in 'Euphrosyne', one of Goethe's greatest poems.

'Lass nicht ungerühmt mich zu den Schatten hinabgehn!
Nur die Muse gewährt einiges Leben dem Tod . . .

Bildete doch ein Dichter auch mich; und seine Gesänge,
Ja, sie vollenden an mir, was mir das Leben versagt.' —
Also sprach sie, und noch bewegte der liebliche Mund
sich,
Weiter zu reden; allein schwirrend versagte der Ton.
Denn aus dem Purpurgewölk, dem schwebenden, immer
bewegten,
Trat der herrliche Gott Hermes gelassen hervor.

The wish of the dead to be given the reality of remembered presence, the curiously whirring sound of the shadow eager, but no longer able, to speak — all this is here superbly rendered in mythological images.

The metaphor of silence, so central in his lyric poetry, is a no less telling ingredient of Goethe's dramatic work. We remember the tactical silences of the early plays: coy in *Die Laune des Verliebten*; a sign of indecision in *Die Mitschuldigen*; the silences of intrigue and deception in *Götz*; Clavigo's agonized silence during Beaumarchais's accusations; Stella's account of her first encounter with Fernando — 'In den seligsten Augenblicken schwiegen wir und verstanden uns . . . nun lasst mich schweigen und ruhen.' All these are not merely the devices of conventional theatrical suspense; they are moments of emotional intensity beyond speech. Egmont's openness is contrasted with the devious silences of his opponents: he stands silent 'in sich versenkt' as he receives his judgment. Tasso's respectful silence before his patron — 'Dein heilig Wort verehrend, /Heiss ich mein innres Herz im tiefsten schweigen' — turns ultimately into that cry of insufferable pain, that anguished silence of which only the poet is able to speak. Iphigenie's silence is the token of her fateful secret. It is not easily revealed:

> Vom alten Bande löset ungern sich
> Die Zunge los, ein langverschwiegenes
> Geheimnis endlich zu entdecken. Denn
> Einmal vertraut, verlässt es ohne Rückkehr
> Des tiefen Herzens sichre Wohnung . . .   (I, 3)

The silences between her and Thoas remain a bond, more often implied than stated: the groping gestures of a human relationship that might, at moments, relieve the stern compulsion of mythical secrecy and obedience.

In *Faust* there are few scenes which are not accented, or given momentary focus, by the uncertainty of speech; by suspension or withholding in awe or surprise, in shock or anticipation: Faust's silence in Auerbach's Cellar, before the magic mirror; in Margarete's room or in agony at her state of mind in the dungeon. The images of speech failing or, at the Emperor's court, perverted, form the links in a chain of Protean ambiguity, of mishearing and misnaming. Helen's encounter with the silent monstrosity of Phorkyas, her inability to speak — 'denn das Wort bemüht / Sich nur umsonst, Gestalten schöpferisch aufzubaun'; the chorus imploring Phorkyas to cease his denigration of Helen — 'Schweige, schweige! / Missblickende, Missredende du!'; Lynkeus, the incarnation of living speech, overwhelmed by the approach of

Helen and, later, silenced in the face of that wanton destruction
which the ancient couple Philemon and Baucis can only face in
silent ritual — 'Lasst uns läuten, knieen, beten / Und dem alten
Gott vertraun!': these are but a few of the episodic signals of the
failure of speech — countermanded by the grand affirmation of
the Word in Chiron's account of Hercules and Helen; or in the
joining of Faust and Helen; or as the instrument of revelation, of
indentification and praise, in the lyrical ecstasies of the concluding
scene.

IV

Language — grandly asserted, and mysteriously intensified or
illuminated in symbols and allegories of silence — makes *Faust* a
document of incomparable poetic power. Yet Goethe's fascination
with the phenomenon and metaphor of silence is nowhere more
richly and explicitly demonstrated than in his narrative work. The
incidental elaboration in his lyrical or dramatic statements
assumes in his fiction the scope of thematic and figurative
concentration. In this mode alone, the topic is unfolded in all its
ramifications. We can observe the impact upon those involved in
silent performance; as partisans, we ourselves are drawn into a
complexity and compulsion, to which we must bring both
understanding and sympathy. We share the state of mind of the
hero of his exquisite *Novelle*, Honorio, when at the end of his
impetuous day he looks, lost in thought, towards the setting sun;
aware, it seems, even before her words are uttered, of the old
woman's advice: 'säume nicht, du wirst überwinden'. Absorbed
in silent recollection, he is the epitome of quiet resolve: 'eine
rötliche Sonne überschien sein Gesicht, sie glaubte nie einen
schönern Jüngling gesehen zu haben'. His moment of silence
seems to offer, as prospect and retrospect, a key to the whole
work.

In *Wilhelm Meisters Lehrjahre*, a narrative of remarkable imaginative
and rhetorical profusion, silence is one of the ritualistic precepts
of that 'Society of the Tower' which guides Wilhelm through a
succession of baffling incidents. The intense inwardness of
Mignon is dramatized in the curiously private signs, which she
offers to Wilhelm in devout obedience to a fateful charge. Like
that of Ottilie in *Die Wahlverwandtschaften*, her silence is made

fascinatingly ominous as a state of mind that has both a pathological and a more awesome dimension. She expresses her feelings most directly in music: 'Nur mit Worten konnte es (*sic*) sich nicht ausdrücken, und es schien das Hindernis mehr in seiner Denkungsart als in den Sprachwerkzeugen zu liegen.'

> Manche Tage war sie ganz stumm, zuzeiten antwortete sie mehr auf verschiedene Fragen, immer sonderbar, doch so, dass man nicht unterscheiden konnte, ob es Witz oder Unkenntis der Sprache war, indem sie ein gebrochnes mit Französisch und Italienisch durch-flochtenes Deutsch sprach.   (GA, VII, 117)

It is however in Goethe's last two novels, *Die Wahlverwandtschaften* and *Wilhelm Meisters Wanderjahre*, that the metaphor of silence is most impressively elaborated, and integrated into the fictional design. In the former it is an evident part of the symbolic machinery: from the moment that Ottilie, the strangely awkward and passive central figure of the novel, arrives in the aristocratic household which she is doomed fatally to disrupt, she strikes Eduard as agreeable and entertaining. 'Unterhaltend?' his wife asks; 'sie hat ja den Mund noch nicht aufgetan.' Throughout the novel this most naive and vulnerable of Goethe's characters finds herself drawn into the destructive element of love; as she becomes aware of her role in a drama of subliminal emotional logic, she rejects food and refuses to speak. Her instinctive discretion is rendered in pointed indications of reticence; on the rare occasions when she wishes to decline a request she does so:

> ... mit einer Gebärde, die für den, der den Sinn davon gefasst hat, unwiderstehlich ist. Sie drückt die flachen Hände, die sie in die Höhe hebt, zusammen und führt sie gegen die Brust, indem sie sich nur wenig vorwärts neigt und den dringend Fordernden mit einem solchen Blick ansieht, dass er gern von allem absteht, was er verlangen oder wünschen möchte.   (GA, IX, 49f.)

Ottilie's silences represent one pole of that scale of intention and failure of which the exorbitant loquaciousness of other characters and the calculated detachment in the narrator's voice may represent the other.

With its extraordinary tensions between a disciplined surface and strong undercurrents of passion and wilfulness, between decorum and its jeopardy as the result of forces beyond social convention, *Elective Affinities* is a masterpiece of structural and rhetorical purity as well as of deliberate ambiguity. And it is not surprising that such interlocking of carefully measured narrative prose and the ultimate assertion of silence should have resulted in strikingly discrepant interpretations. Ottilie's refusal to speak has been taken as an indication of her desire to atone for her part in the dissolution of a sacred premise of the social order. But the emblematic ending of the novel, with its reiterated gestures of muteness, may suggest not so much a quasi-religious resolution of the narrated conflicts through Ottilie's self-imposed penance as her incapacity to act maturely and responsibly. Her final surrender to absolute silence is, at any rate, the sum of an eloquently joined series of events, conversations, hints and turns of phrase through which Goethe seeks to juxtapose the power of a narrator of sovereign linguistic and technical command and the disruption of social discipline and responsibility by uncontrolled, perhaps uncontrollable, natural forces that undermine the assumptions of civilized communication.

This reality of instinctive forces unbalancing a precariously maintained social order gives way in *Wilhelm Meisters Wanderjahre* to the overriding importance of ritual as the premise of community. It is a novel which counters Goethe's earlier belief in the ability of the individual to realize an inherent capacity for acculturation. What now requires understanding is the preponderance of collective and social pressures. The novel is therefore above all a fictional elaboration of the relationship between information or knowledge and its organization or preservation in institutions. The thematic recurrence of the motifs of ignorance and insight lends to the *Wanderjahre* its narrative pattern: the give and take between inquiry and didactic response; the suspense caused by events barely understood or mysterious; their gradual, but eventual, elucidation. To draw attention to surprising or disturbing emotional relationships is, therefore, one of the important postures of the narrator, who repeatedly declares his implication in such phrases as 'Hier nun müssen wir vertraulich eröffnen', or 'wir müssen ein Geheimeres offenbaren'. Speech and silence are in this deliberately involuted novel elaborately intertwined as attitudes, not only in the characters, but in the narrator too. It is these which produce the variations in the narration, and are then paraphrased as explicit themes in the intercalated novellas. Thus it is secretiveness and silence which propel the action of 'Joseph der Zweite'; in 'Der Mann von fünfzig Jahren' the account of the love of father and son for the same girl culminates in a silent encounter of unsurpassed intensity, in which the three 'Verirrten, Verwirrten' recognize their dilemma; there is 'Wirrwarr ohne Grenzen' in the tale 'Nicht zu Weit', in which the wife finds her lover in love with one of her friends. The sudden discovery of this furtive relationship leaves her more in pensive silence than display: 'Albertine stand vor sich hinschauend, einzeln, kaum bemerkt.' The ritual of silence, whether in work or reflection, as a means of indicating that threefold reverence for what is above, below and within us, is one of the conditions of life among the children in the 'Pedagogic Province'. The figure of Makarie, 'die schweigsamste aller Frauen', who lives in a state of serene contemplation of the universe, is as much a symbolic representation of the congruence of insight, and its intimation in gestures of utmost inwardness, as is Mignon. In one of the most romantic incidents of the novel a talented painter presents a picture of this 'anmutige Scheinknabe' to Wilhelm and his friends who are visiting the magic Italian setting of Mignon's early life. The recollection of that paradoxical child, 'in sich gekehrt ohne Trutz, unwillig ohne Widerstreben', is orchestrated in intensely lyrical passsages. 'Kennst du das Land . . .' — that first 'Zartgesang des holden Kindes' — is once more intoned; the deep emotions of the listeners are joined in silence.

This late and last novel is a work of fiction as irregular in its techniques as it is rich in indications of Goethe's unceasing efforts at testing the scope of language in alternating movements of narrative and discourse. And more than any other of his works it displays 'Entsagung' as the variously encoded formula for Goethe's abiding sense of discretion in conduct no less than in the use of language. It is a term which points to his acceptance of the finite nature of insight; and at the same time to the compulsion of the poet, in an act of saying, to do justice to the evident abundance of the experienced world as well as to its tantalizing inscrutability. In the pursuit of such a purpose, speech and silence are bound to be closely linked modes. Far from carrying a connotation of resignation or vacuity, the metaphor of silence is here, as throughout Goethe's work, one of the mirrors of consciousness that may show us the enchanting and elusive configurations of life.

It was, perhaps, with a sly and playful hint at the creative interdependence of silence and speech in his own art that he inserted the episode of the silent barber who performs his task with great skill but without uttering a word. He smiles when he is asked to give a reason: 'Schalkhaft lächelnd, den Finger auf den Mund legend, schlich der Schweigsame zur Türe hinaus'. Forty pages later his secret is revealed: he had come to dislike the garrulousness of his trade and had imposed upon himself the denial of casual speech.

> Dieser also hat nun auf die Sprache Verzicht getan, insofern etwas Gewöhnliches, oder Zufälliges durch sie ausgedrückt wird; daraus aber hat sich ihm ein anderes Redetalent entwickelt, welches absichtlich, klug und erfreulich wirkt, die Gabe des Erzählens nämlich. Sein Leben ist reich an wunderlichen Erfahrungen, die er sonst zu ungelegener Zeit schwätzend zersplitterte, nun aber durch Schweigen genötigt im stillen Sinne wiederholt und ordnet. Hiermit verbindet sich denn die Einbildungskraft und verleiht dem Geschehenen Leben und Bewegung. Mit besonderer Kunst und Geschicklichkeit weiss er wahrhafte Märchen und märchenhafte Geschichten zu erzählen. (GA, VIII, 339, 379)

Of such complex awareness may be born even the loquaciousness and discretions, the garrulity and silences, of barbers and artists alike.

Notes to The Metaphor of Silence

1. The same impulse to reticence as expressed by the hero in Goethe's first draft of *Wilhelm Meister*; 'Wilhelm Meisters Theatralische Sendung', II, 3-5. But how much refined by a lifetime's experience!

2. From his review of a manual of Church History by J.T.L. Danz in 1826; GA, XIV, 358.

Man of the Theatre   Walter Hinck

That Shakespeare was a man of the theatre, that Molière was too, these are the sort of facts one learns at school. For Raimund and Nestroy, as still for Wedekind and Brecht, the theatre was a workshop: it was where they earned their living. They were bound to it by profession as well as by calling.

But Goethe? Member of the Government of the Grand Duchy of Saxe-Weimar (member even of its 'Geheimes Consilium'), War Commissioner, Director of Road Works, and President of the Chamber of Finance — can this Goethe, Weimar Minister of State, also be hailed as a man of the theatre? True, the young reigning Duke, Charles Augustus, entrusted to the young poet he had persuaded to settle in Weimar in 1776 the direction of an amateur theatre: members of his Court, including Goethe and the young Duke himself, appeared there, together with a few professional actors. And between 1791 and 1817 Goethe, in addition to his other public duties, held the office of Director of the Court theatre. But it was unpaid work; a subsidiary activity. Theatre director, minister, scientist, poet, the major representative of a whole epoch in so many fields — can Goethe really be proclaimed as 'man of the theatre' in the full sense of this term?

Such a question is not to be answered through Goethe's dramatic works alone. Although to him suitability for the stage was one of the main requirements of any drama. He said in a conversation with Eckermann on 4 February 1829:

> Writing for the theatre is a quite peculiar sort of thing; and if you don't understand the business from start to

> finish, you'd best leave it alone . . . Things may read very
> well on the page and be very nice to think about in one's
> thoughts. But seen on stage they're a quite different kettle
> of fish. What may have enchanted us in a book can leave
> us utterly cold in the theatre.

And he made no exception of his youthful play, *Götz von
Berlichingen*, or his own later adaptations thereof. In an earlier
conversation with Eckermann on 26 July 1826 he had said:

> A play which is not conceived and designed for the stage
> right from the start will not subsequently prove playable
> thereon; whatever you do with it there will always remain
> an unmanageable, a resistant element. The trouble I took
> with my own *Götz von Berlichingen*! Yet even to this day it is
> not completely convincing on stage.

Clearly Goethe was not prepared to champion the written drama,
the poetic text, against the demands of the stage: this was the acid
test and not every dramatic work stood up to it. Even Shakespeare's
plays, as we shall see, were not in his view always entirely suitable
for the stage. Of course Goethe was judging by the specific
conditions of the particular theatre he had to work in. But the very
fact that he did judge by such conditions shows him to be a man of
the theatre indeed.

   Is there not however an apparent contradiction to what I have
just said in the work which he began as a novel of the theatre and
finished as a 'Bildungsroman', namely *Wilhelm Meister*? When he
resumed work on the novel after his two Italian journeys (to be
more precise in 1791) did Goethe not actually move away from
the theatre, by relinquishing the first draft of that novel which he
had entitled 'Wilhelm Meister's Theatrical Mission' and assimilating
its contents into a whole new concept of education for life, namely
Wilhelm Meister's Years of Apprenticeship? We cannot of course simply
identify the author with the main character of his novel. But the
shift in focus precisely during the years after his appointment as
Director of the Court theatre is striking. In the 'Theatralische
Sendung' the child's experiences with puppets and puppet plays
are not recalled as reminiscences, but narrated directly: we are
given a realistic picture of his experiences and experiments in the
world of the theatre, and Wilhelm's path to the foundation of a
German 'national theatre' is clearly marked out. In the *Apprenticeship*

Years this productive encounter with the theatre remains an episode; a transition stage in an overall educational plan in which art may well prove a valuable means but can never be the ultimate aim. It is as if Goethe had created for himself in the fictional world of his newly conceived novel a counterweight to the closer ties he himself had now made with the real world of the theatre. Art itself would now appear to serve as an essential corrective to any concern with art. On the other hand, we cannot ignore the fact that Goethe's public and administrative duties would in any case have prevented his unconditional involvement in the theatre. So that his new conception of *Wilhelm Meister* may be said to represent a certain distancing from practical problems of theatre just at a time when they were threatening to engulf him. In other words: Goethe never gave himself to the stage body and soul. He was never more than a man of the theatre part-time. If when young this Goethe of many forms was often referred to as Proteus, the older Goethe was no less Protean either. But in a different way. His many offices and tasks then forced him into different roles. And this constant variety and change seemed to impart to his existence something of the quality of an actor's. And just one of the many roles he played in all seriousness was that of man of the theatre.

Not only as manager, or artistic director. Although in this function too he had to take decisions of vital importance: he had, for instance, to decide on the repertoire. But this office also brought with it many tedious tasks which taxed his patience beyond the point where it could contain his irritation. The history of Goethe's direction of the Weimar theatre is not just a list of creditable items. Let us be quite frank. Goethe the theatre director occasionally behaved like an autocrat: whether towards the literary public; or towards the theatre audience; or even towards the actors themselves. When the headmaster of the local grammar school, K.A. Böttiger, who was an occasional contributor to literary journals run by Goethe and Schiller, produced a satirical review of the producton of August Wilhelm Schlegel's *Ion* for the *Journal des Luxus und der Moden,* Goethe threatened to resign and insisted that in future all reviews of theatrical productions should be shown to him before publication. While his peremptory 'No laughter, please!' when calling an unruly audience to order during a performance of Friedrich Schlegel's *Alarcos* in that same year, 1802, has become notorious. Measures he took against the eighteen-year-old actress, Wilhelmine Maas, who had given a guest performance in Berlin without first obtaining permission, and was put under house arrest for a week after her return to Weimar, is hardly a laughing matter either: not only did Goethe position a sentry outside her door, he made the poor girl pay for this punishment herself!

But if he occasionally over-disciplined the members of his company, imposing what may seem to us a far too severe regime on them, Goethe also raised their social standing. Under his directorship the actors entered formally into the service of the court; and this brought them financial security. By 1820 the income of one of the singers and five of the actors was on the same level as, or even higher than, the salary paid to Privy Councillors of the Government; and it was actually higher than that of the Bürgermeister and the Duke's own surgeon.[1] During Goethe's directorship the social position of the theatre personnel improved markedly. If absolutism was one face of the patriarchal relationship between the director and the members of his company, his concern for their welfare was the other.

In the court theatres of nineteenth-century Germany directors, especially if they came from the aristocracy, usually restricted themselves to administrative work. In the modern theatre most directors are also producers, and they reserve the right to produce some of the plays in the repertoire themselves. Goethe, too, would hardly have found the task of theatre management attractive had it not given him the opportunity for artistic work, for the theatrical realization of his own ideas. His stage designs — for Mozart's *Magic Flute*, for instance — have survived. They show a remarkable talent for the visual arts. The directions for movement in his productions also draw directly on the visual arts. His main interest in the theatre was certainly in working with actors. Social conventions prevented the Minister for the Arts from himself appearing as a performer on the Weimar stage once it had become professional. But Goethe's acting ability proved its worth in rehearsals, where he could not only explain his view of a role but actually demonstrate what he meant. During the period in which he worked with Schiller on productions —that is during the years 1799 to 1805, after Schiller's move from Jena to Weimar — Goethe preferred to handle the movements and choreography and leave the details of the production to Schiller.

His 'Rules for Actors' — instructions on pronunciation, recitation, declamation and grouping on the stage — are the product of practical work in the theatre. Goethe keeps his company on a very tight rein. To the unprepared reader the 'Rules for Actors' may seem more like military drill. They are clearly stamped by the behavioural conventions of court society. But there is also an analogy to dance. This is a codification of instructions which were only intended for rehearsals with a particular ensemble; they were to perfect a style specific to one place and one time. In them the tradition of the Court theatre at Weimar and the aesthetics of Weimar classicism meet; the neo-classicism of Goethe's approach to production is imposed on a Baroque instrument. If raised to the level of a law these 'Rules for Actors' reveal the transitory nature of all theatrical art, its dependence upon a particular time and place. It is not only in the perspective of 'realistic' or 'naturalistic' drama that Goethe's instructions on speech and movement seem alien to us: a wide gap separates this very artificial, measured, statuesque approach from any modern concept at all. While the plays of the Weimar classical period have held their own in the repertoire, the style of producing them on stage seems irrevocably a thing of the past: historical —with all that this implies. Knowledge of Goethe's 'technical-grammatical' instructions to his actors is of no use whatsoever in any modern production of either his own or of Schiller's plays. That is one of the hard truths which my subject — 'Goethe, Man of the Theatre' — attempts to come to terms with.

But precisely this law of the temporary and the transient, to which the Weimar concept of theatre was inevitably subject, was also evident to Goethe himself. It was the legitimation of his own production of plays from the classical repertoire, from world literature. Paradoxical as it may sound, it was his awareness of the inevitably historical nature of all theatrical practice that made his own productions exemplary. Of course Goethe's productions are inconceivable without his own activities as dramatist and producer; without his pepping-up of texts (his own included). The producer guides the hand of the dramaturg; but the dramaturg also guides the hand of the producer. If Goethe's mode of production, with its concentration on particular stylistic elements and concrete details, belongs irrevocably to the past, its principles at least have a more contemporary relevance, certainly as a subject of discussion, than might at first appear.

Goethe did not see his theatre as an educative institution: where it did manage to teach and cultivate, then it was to do so imperceptibly. Boredom, even of the most elevated kind, was to him a sin against the living spirit of the theatre. He had no illusions about the expectations of his audience; but he did not despise them either. After the production of Calderon's *The Constant Prince*, one of his most ambitious, and a triumph which gave him great satisfaction, he wrote to Georg Sartorius, Professor of Politics in Göttingen, on 4 February 1811:

> Everything in the theatre . . . depends on freshness of effect. People don't want to reflect, think, or concede. They want to feel and enjoy. That is why minor works often enjoy more success than major ones. And rightly so! But this time we had a play, written nearly two hundred years ago, under a different sky and for an audience with a totally different background; and our performance was as fresh as if it was straight out of the pan.

Leaving aside for a moment the problem Goethe was touching on with his vivid image of a play 'fresh from the pan', we can see that this is a man of the living theatre who was not interested in a culture-vulture audience. He knew that people do not go to the theatre in search of a temple for idle hours; they demand from it too the daily bread of art. And he arranged his repertoire accordingly! Far more so than many of his admirers really care to admit. Nevertheless: many a modern theatre director who conceives his duty as making heavier and heavier demands on his audience might learn from such an unclassical classicist how to achieve an economic balance between education and pleasure, pedagogy and entertainment, relaxation and demands upon the intellect.

Goethe pays his own sort of tribute to his age and its taste. The bourgeois 'family portraits', for which von Gemmingen's *Teutscher Hausvater*, Kotzebue's *Häuslicher Zwist* or Iffland's *Vaterhaus* are appropriate titles, take up a large part of the repertoire. The need for emotion, heir to sensibility, is also met and acknowledged. Of 601 productions between 1791 and 1817 one fifth alone were plays by Kotzebue and Iffland. Romantic fate tragedies were obviously very popular; the production in 1810 of Zacharias Werner's *Der vierundzwanzigste Februar* seemed to Goethe particularly good. There can be no doubt that even in Classical Weimar light literature for the stage held its own.

Anyone who regards this as 'accomodation', or 'conformism', is forgetting that it was at that time the only way of opening up an adequate stage for important contemporary works and making the Weimar theatre a forum for world drama. It was a rare coincidence of German dramatic history, a peak in the development of the German theatre, when Goethe and Schiller took joint responsibility for productions. In the few years of their collaboration the first performances of Schiller's *Maria Stuart, Die Braut von Messina*, his *Wallenstein* trilogy and *Wilhelm Tell*, followed closely upon each other; only the first performance of the *Jungfrau von Orleans* in Leipzig preceded that in Weimar. Plays by Goethe performed between 1799 and 1805 were — in addition to minor works such as *Die Geschwister, Der Bürgergeneral, Jery und Bätely* and *Paläophron —Iphigenie, Götz von Berlichingen* and the early comedies *Die Mitschuldigen* and *Die Laune des Verliebten*. It was a natural result of the interplay between drama and theatre that experience gained in practical production should be directly reflected in textual modifications. It has in fact been shown that the structure of their classical plays was adapted to the conditions obtaining in the theatre around 1800. That Schiller's stage directions, for example, are directly related to stage practice in Weimar.

But this in itself created a problem for Goethe and Schiller as soon as they set about realizing their other aim of establishing the major plays of other ages and countries on the Weimar stage. For in these plays, too, there was a relation — sometimes close, sometimes looser — between the actual dramatic text and versions adapted for any particular production. As a result Goethe and Schiller were, in their efforts to build up a wide repertoire, often faced with a discrepancy between whatever text was available and the possibilities of realizing it on the particular stage at their disposal. Of course any production of plays from past epochs of foreign countries will encounter similar difficulties. But the problem was particularly acute in Weimar because Goethe and Schiller were trying to realize something which

Goethe was later to formulate programmatically: 'National literature does not mean much any more; we are coming to the age of World Literature; and everyone should do his utmost to hasten its realization' (to Eckermann, 31 January 1827). To the particular intensity with which Goethe and Schiller attempted to establish world theatre on the Weimar stage must be added their felt need to put their own experience, their creative energy as dramatists, at the service of the *mise en scène*. In other words to adjust the plays themselves to the stylistic trend of the Weimar Court theatre; to bring them 'close' to the audience in the literal sense of this word. If we run down the list of major dramas which were produced while Goethe was in charge of the theatre we can see how representative the selection was: Sophocles's *Antigone*, Plautus's *Ghost* and four comedies by Terence; Shakespeare's *King John, Hamlet, Henry IV, Macbeth, Julius Caesar,* and *Othello*; Otway's *Venice Preserved*, Corneille's *Le Cid*, Racine's *Mithridate* and *Phèdre*, Molière's *L'Avare* and *Le Docteur Miracle*; Calderon's *The Constant Prince, Life as a Dream*, and *Great Zenobia*; Holberg's *Politischer Kannengiesser* and three comedies by Goldoni, including *The Servant of Two Masters*, Gozzi's *Turandot* in Schiller's adaptation, Voltaire's *Mahomet, Tancred*, and *Zaïre*, Lessing's *Emilia Galotti, Minna von Barnhelm*, and *Nathan*. In the opera repertoire we find Gluck's *Iphigénie en Tauride*, almost all Mozart's operas and Beethoven's *Fidelio*. The structure begins to emerge and —with a few exceptions of course — it has remained the core of the classical repertoire in German theatres to this day. What is all too obvious is just how far German literature lagged behind historically. Whereas the theatre in other West European countries had long acquired a classical repertoire, German dramatic literature did not move from the national to the European level until Lessing. And it does indeed appear as a happy interplay of 'giving' and 'taking' that the two dramatists who finally ensured the break-through of German literature on to a European level themselves built up an exemplary European repertoire in Weimar.

Among the productions during Goethe's management of the theatre was of course Schiller's *Räuber*. Revolutionary enthusiasm on the stage of a court theatre — that could hardly, especially after the French Revolution, be to the taste of court society. And so — just as at the time when Joseph Bellomo and his company played in the Weimer theatre (1784-91) — the Court stayed away. This offers, towards the end of the age of absolutism, a noteworthy example of princely self-restriction, on the one hand, and of artistic integrity, on the other. The Court refrained from exercising any pressure — after all during the '70s a performance of Lessing's *Emilia Galotti* had been banned in neighbouring Gotha — and restricted itself to a gesture of displeasure. But in his capacity as theatre director, Goethe — who was himself bound to court society, not only through his ministerial office, but also through common activity in amateur productions and on festive occasions — was not prepared to keep the play out of the repertoire of his own accord. He did not subject himself to what today is called 'self-censorship'. The unpleasant concept of the 'prince's hireling' was to be forgotten forever.

The complaint is often made today that producers treat dramatic texts arbitrarily, especially the classics, degrading them to the level of mere material with which to gain superficial effects. The objection is justified, indeed it is neccesary, where there is not artistic justification for either intervention or superimposition. But where should the line be drawn? The doctrine of the sanctity of the word, especially the word of established classics, is always a dubious argument in the theatre. Certainly our own classical writers, Goethe and Schiller, did not show such unconditional respect for the texts which had been handed down to them.

It is the task of producer and actors alike to present the play to the audience as if — to use Goethe's image again —it had come 'fresh from the pan'. That is quite a task even with a modern play. And it is very difficult indeed with plays in the classical repertoire. The history of the Weimar Court theatre under Goethe is not by any means just a story of successes. It is well known, for instance, that he had a failure with Kleist's *Zerbrochener Krug*: that his production of 1808, with its mistaken division into three acts, destroyed the structure of that comedy and would have been far better without the long variant reading. But, on the other hand, Goethe accepted Schiller's rigorous treatment of his own *Egmont* in 1796, although in retrospect, in his essay 'On the German Theatre' which appeared in 1818, he could not suppress the comment that Schiller had 'cut the play down cruelly'. On the other hand again, he himself was no less cruel in his own adaptation of other plays, as we can see from the example of the

Weimar version of *Romeo and Juliet* in 1812.

This was the last of Schiller and Goethe's adaptations of Shakespeare's plays. And it was certainly the most far-reaching and controversial. At the same time it was also most characteristic of Goethe's own literary practice in the theatre. Schiller's adaptations of *Macbeth* and *Othello*, like Goethe's handling of *King John, Hamlet, Henry IV* and *King Lear*, follow a principle which Goethe formulated in his essay 'Über das deutsche Theater' when outlining Schiller's dramaturgical plans: 'The main material, the essential content of the work should be brought into a form which is appropriate partly for the stage itself and partly for the sense and spirit of the present age.' They both followed this principle carefully, mainly damping down the element of spectacle in that tradition of German Shakespeare productions which goes back to the time of the wandering players in the seventeenth century. Goethe thought he could discern enough spectacle in Shakespeare's own text — even in *Romeo and Juliet*. His comments on his own adaptation and production of this play, for instance, are to be found in a letter to Caroline von Wolzogen of 28 January 1812:

> The maxim I followed was to intensify what is of interest and bring it all into harmony; since Shakespeare, following his genius, the spirit of his age and the wishes of his audience was prone to bring together a great deal of disharmonious stuff; indeed he had to do this in order to please the theatre-goers of his time.

What Goethe meant by 'disharmonious stuff' — 'Allotria' — was firstly the rough comic and obscene scenes and dialogues which seemed to the neo-classical spirit a disruptive element, not in keeping with the principle of purity of genre, and infringing the basic tragic mood. It should not be forgotten that the Weimar theatre, like other theatres of the time, was very much under the pressure of non-artistic, of purely social conventions. Erotic and sexual elements in particular (like church and state, if for different reasons) were taboo on stage. In his adaptations of *Macbeth* Schiller replaced the porter's 'indecent' jokes with a pious morning song. And Goethe frequently complained about the excessive sensibility he was expected to show. As, for instance, in his conversation with Eckermann of 29 January 1826. The latter suggested that the 'excessive sensibility' of the audience was due to literary influences. 'No', replied Goethe, 'it comes from society itself. And what are all these young girls doing in the theatre anyway? They don't belong there at all! They should be in a convent. The theatre is only for men and women who are familiar with human affairs.' Goethe's irritation on this point would certainly not suit the feminists among us. But it cannot be used as an argument against the emancipation of women either. For it is directed precisely against the contradiction between a convent upbringing and the reality expressed on stage.

By 'Allotria' Goethe might also mean scenes and dialogues which distracted attention from the main idea or interrupted the action: in other words ran counter to the classical aim of a manifest unity in the whole. Goethe was always concerned with what he called 'stationary' effects; and in this respect even his re-working of his own *Götz* in 1804 still seemed unsatisfactory to him. 'The fluid historical progression certainly prevents the scenes from having any stationary interest; and this, after all, is what is required in the theatre' (*Tag- und Jahreshefte*, 1804; WA, i, XXXV, 186). His adaptation of *Romeo and Juliet* sacrifices twelve out of twenty-four changes of scene to such 'stationary effects'. In the Shakespeare productions, by contrast with the adaptations of French plays, alterations were necessary not least because of the limited physical possibilities of the Weimar stage. As a proscenium this differed fundamentally from the three-tiered structure used by Shakespeare which, with its 'simultaneous' effect had such marked influence on his plays.' In Weimar scenic mobility was very much more restricted, especially since the stage itself was so small (11.61 metres wide, 9. 21 metres deep, with an opening of a little over 7 metres, and just on 6.5 metres high).

However, the extent of his changes to *Romeo and Juliet* can hardly be explained by the dimensions of the stage. Of the translation by Schlegel Goethe used two thirds (and even this not without alterations to the language), but scarcely one tenth of the first act. This was not only to shorten the play: quite often new passages replaced the cuts. The exposition, the quarrel between the servants which reflects the quarrel between the houses of Montague and Capulet, is removed and replaced by an idyllic 'Singspiel' and a masked procession. The nurse is domesticated; the witty and refreshing Mercutio virtually resembles Falstaff.

The tragedy does not end with a reconciliation of the heads of the families, but with the death of Juliet — and a final address, a succession of admonitory aphorisms.

Such an adaptation may well be called an ill-judged operation, an amputation. Goethe himself anticipated the criticism. On 21 February 1812 he wrote to his publisher, Cotta: 'The play is not suitable for publication; nor would I wish to deliver up to devoted translators and conservers of Shakespeare something on which they can expend all their conceit.' It was not only conceit which raised a protesting voice; whether among scholars of Shakespeare or of Goethe himself. One of the harshest judgments comes from W.H. Bruford (*Theatre, Drama and Audience*, p. 319): 'Perhaps the least creditable of all Goethe's productions was his amazing travesty of *Romeo and Juliet.*' But do not such verdicts overlook the style of the Weimar stage and the consensus which was achieved by paying attention to the expectations of the contemporary audience? The establishment of world literature, in this case of the most famous love tragedy, in the contemporary theatre, transcends literary and even scholarly considerations. Goethe is only concerned to meet the requirements of his own theatre. We do not have to approve of every change he made. But we do not have to echo every criticism either.

Goethe takes the core of the play, the love tragedy, very seriously. And he sees this tragic core as jeopardized by the comic figures of Mercutio and the nurse and many another 'foreign element'. We may regret his cutting of the final scene, the reconciliation. But Goethe, who considered himself too conciliant by nature for a truly tragic poet, had a rather strict view of tragedy: 'All tragedy is based on an irreconcilable opposition. The moment that reconciliation puts in an appearance, or even appears possible, the tragic element is destroyed' (to Kanzler von Müller, 6 July 1824).There can be no doubt that the reconciliation scene in *Romeo and Juliet*, even if it comes too late for the lovers, adds a softer note to the basically tragic mood. It is not actually the premature end to the action that is inconsistent, but rather the obvious moralizing of the final maxims.

The fact that what is left is only a truncated version of Shakespeare's text, the adapter claiming poetic licence for a larger part of this stage version, was not seen by Goethe as a fault. The theatre bill for the first performance, on 1 February 1812, announced: '*Romeo and Juliet*, a tragedy in five acts, by Goethe, after Shakespeare and Schlegel'. This is an honest way of preventing false expectations and taking responsibility for the new work. Modern producers rarely shun 'Allotria'; indeed they are more likely to add a bit more, even to Shakespeare. And it would be a welcome change indeed if the adapter or producer were always to put his name to any far-reaching changes he makes. Hansgünther Heyme was one of the few who did. His 1969 version of *Wallenstein* in Cologne changed the structure of the trilogy completely, and the book of that production was published by Suhrkamp under the joint authorship of Schiller/ Heyme.

If Goethe did not want any toning down of the tragic element in *Romeo and Juliet*, and hence cut the elements of family feuding and reconciliation, the harmonization of which he himself spoke did not affect the love story itself: on the contrary, it is precisely this that his version emphasizes. What is 'brought into harmony' is everything offered on stage to the sense perception of the audience. The opening coronation scene and masked procession in the style of 'Singspiel' which Goethe introduced into the first act indicate the direction he was aiming at. What has been added to the original is designed to please eye and ear. The influence of opera and musical theatre upon the style of movement used on the Weimar stage, even in plays which made no use of music at all, is well known. For the rest it is the laws of painting which determine the choreographic approach. In Paragraph 85 of his 'Rules for Actors' Goethe calls the stage a 'scenic picture'. That is in keeping with his fondness for 'living tableaux', the grouping of real persons to resemble a painted scene (see 'Über Proserpina', 1815; WA, i, XL, 117).

We know how important an organ the eye was to Goethe. If he agreed to remain Director of the Theatre for a good quarter of a century, even after he had insisted on relinquishing other ministerial offices, and despite many a quarrel, even with the Duke, and the growing burden of other duties, it was in large degree due to the fact that the theatre is basically a visual art. The dramatist's words there take on visible form. Admittedly he was only prepared to accept a visual art which does not betray the absolute standards of human being and the human spirit. In the notorious affair which caused his resignation, when the play

Aubry de Mont-Didier's Dog or the Woods near Bondy was performed, against his will, on 12 April 1817 with a trained dog as the star attraction, he saw these standards in his view shamefully infringed. Goethe's only answer to the invasion of the theatre by the circus was to withdraw from the theatre itself.

And there was no going back. 'I was only', he said to Eckermann on 29 January 1826, 'really interested in the theatre as long as I could do practical work there. It was my joy and pleasure to raise that institution to a higher level . . . But now that I can no longer have any practical influence I feel no call to go there any more.' We do not necessarily have to regret this lack of interest in any further developments in the Weimar theatre. For it did not in fact mean a breach with the art itself. It was merely the other side of a new, more productive, preoccupation with the theatre: what the Weimar stage lost through Goethe's withdrawal the Second Part of *Faust* gained. Indeed, *Faust II* may well be seen as splendid compensation for the end of Goethe's practical work as theatre manager, dramaturg, producer and stage designer.

But without his many years of work with actors; without the knowledge he had gained of the needs of the audience; without the experience that all intellectual content must take on visual form in the theatre — that great and profound spectacle would have been totally different. It is not until the Second Part of *Faust* that this experience fully enters into the dramatic text. The step from the First to the Second Part represents the author's progress through practical work in the theatre. This is what L.A. Willoughby had in mind when he says in his 1949 lecture on 'A Morphological Approach to *Faust*' that words, images, metaphors from the First Part turn into full-blown dramatic personages in the Second.[3] When companies do have the courage to tackle this work, a 'world theatre' in itself, it becomes apparent that the highest and most sublime intellectual concept on the one hand, and 'a delight for eye and ear' as Werner Keller has put it,[4] are not mutually exclusive: they enter into a symbiosis. Allegorical masked processions; dance and choric groupings; invocation and transformation scenes; a living mythology; fabulous archaic beings and deities; evil spirits and fantastic hermaphrodites — as well as the incarnation of beauty herself: a veritable cornucopia of symbols. But all in visible form. A multiplicity of metrical forms and rhythms; an endless variety of speech; an enthralling interaction of language, music and a panorama of different worlds — this is the creative sum of decades of living theatre. *Faust II* is the crown of Goethe's artistic achievement; and it will always remain inexhaustible, defying any 'final' interpretation. But it is *at the same time* a second birth of the old Faust play out of the living spirit of the theatre.

Of course it cannot be overlooked that in conceiving this play Goethe went far beyond what he himself had achieved on the Weimar stage, or ever could be achieved on that stage at all. But a discrepancy between the dramatic work itself and any possibilities of staging it was not in Goethe's eyes a misfortune. In his essay 'Shakespeare und kein Ende', published in 1815/16, he argued that Shakespeare's name and achievement belongs to the history of *poetry*, and that his players were not merely a part of the history of theatre. Shakespeare achieves his effects, he maintained, through the living word; and this could always be transmitted more effectively through a reading of his works than through any representation on stage. We can interpret this comment — which must appear strange in view of all his own efforts to put Shakespeare's plays on stage — as meaning that Shakespeare appeals first and foremost to the imagination. But lurking behind it are his doubts about any possibility of ever really doing justice to Shakespeare on stage, and a desire maybe to justify his own adaptations. He shows a more relaxed attitude in his discussion of Ludwig Tieck's dramaturgical writings, the first two volumes of which appeared in 1825/26. There he actually welcomes attempts to perform Shakespeare's plays without any major cuts or changes, although he doubts the possibility of success.

Goethe's style of staging plays has its place in the history of theatre and it could never be revived. Where it did become a model outside Weimar, and after Goethe's death, as in Karl Immermann's 'Exemplary Theatre' in Düsseldorf, it already bore the stigma of the epigonic. But his postulation of mutual encouragement between dramatist, dramaturg and producer has remained exemplary. Goethe's concept of theatre makes drama at home on the stage and the theatre at home in drama. And if one bears in mind Goethe's views on theatrical illusion, a bridge is recognizable from the Weimar theatre, through the proscenium stage of the nineteenth century, to the various stage types used in the twentieth.

These views on 'illusion' are mainly to be found in his report on 'Women's Parts Played by Men in the Roman Theatre' written in 1788 during his Italian Journey. Goethe saw in Roman comedies this custom which had survived from ancient times, and he assesses its advantages as well as its disadvantages. The audience of course is always aware that the roles are being played by men. Nevertheless, Goethe argues, this does not entirely destroy the illusion as an unskilled performance by third or fourth-rate actors — in other words, an inartistic approach — would do. This is where acting differs from pure imitation; here we have an artist playing a 'third, and in fact wholly foreign, nature. But we come to know this "third nature" all the better because someone has observed it, thought it through and presented us, not with the thing itself, but with the result of all this work'. Goethe asks himself why he found such pleasure in the performance, and reaches the conclusion 'that in such an "imitation" the concept of art still remained a living one, and skilful "play" simply produced a kind of self-conscious illusion'.

This is reminiscent of Moses Mendelssohn's view that only full awareness of the fact that it is illusion creates aesthetic pleasure. But it also points forward to Brecht's aesthetic writings on theatre which were directed against the idea of illusion on stage. Of course we can hardly identify Goethe's concept of art with Brecht's. And we scarcely need to discuss here what separates them. But that eighteenth-century traveller to Italy saw much of what Brecht's alienation effect is aimed at: namely, the creation of distance between the actor and his role; the presentation of a 'foreign nature'; the representation of an artistic result as an inherent part of theatre practice. And this became Goethe's model for his own aesthetic theory. What Goethe and Brecht have in common in their vision of the theatre is the departure from a simple 'imitation of nature' and a desire to make theatrical illusion wholly transparent.

But Brecht only underlines principles which have become generally established in the German theatre during the last half century. To this extent — and in defiance of historical chronology — the epoch of the naturalist illusionistic stage (e.g. Otto Brahms) and the magical illusionary theatre (e.g. Max Reinhardt) are further from us than Goethe's theatre, the theatre of 'frank and honest' illusion.

Translated from the German by Eileen Martin and Elizabeth M. Wilkinson.

Notes to Man of the Theatre

1. Heinrich Huesmann, 'Goethe als Theaterleiter. Historisches Umfeld und Grundzüge', in *Ein Theatermann. Theorie und Praxis. Festschrift zum 70. Geburtstag von Rolf Badenhausen,* edited by Ingrid Nohl (Munich, 1977), pp. 143-60 (p. 145).

2. Heinrich Huesmann, *Shakespeare-Inszenierungen unter Goethe in Weimar,* Sitzungsberichte der Österreichischen Akademie der Wissenschaften, Philosophische-historische Klasse, 258 (Vienna, 1968), p. 49.

3. Reprinted in: *Goethe. Poet and Thinker*, pp. 95-117.

4. Werner Keller, 'Das Drama Goethes', in *Handbuch des deutschen Dramas,* edited by Walter Hinck (Düsseldorf, 1980), pp. 133-56.

Note on the Genesis of Sexual Attitudes in Goethe's Life and Works

Since the appearance in 1978 of Siegfried Unseld's admirable edition of 'Das Tagebuch', in a volume to celebrate No. 1000 of the Insel-Bücherei, I have received numerous queries about the statement in Note 41 (p. 182) that circa 1968 I had given an as yet unpublished lecture on that poem in English: Had it not been in German? And on a far wider theme? And was the date not 1967? Neither Dr Unseld nor his informant, Siegfried Sudhof, can be held responsible for misinformation. They took the trouble to enquire of me whether it had meanwhile been published. And if all I could muster in reply was a hastily scrawled 'No! and I doubt it ever will be', this was because their letter caught me at a grievous time. Both confusion and exactitude of date are easily explained. The year 1968 is associated with student violence; my German lecture tour the previous June coincided with silent marches protesting against the shooting by Berlin police of the student Benno Ohnesorg. What painfully embarrassed me was that all I had on offer was such a frivolous-sounding theme. I need not have worried! They took it with a grave attention to its joys and sorrows, and a ready alertness to my ironies and play. And yes! the lecture was in German. Though, foxingly, the title was in English. For the simple reason that — as an appreciative review by Gerda Neumann in the *Göttinger Tageblatt* of 10 June 1967 made clear — my play with 'positions' as an immediately attractive, but ultimately untenable, rendering formed a light-hearted introduction to weightier considerations. 'Das Tagebuch' (or 'The Dairy' as printers sometimes prefer) only made its appearance at the end. It was not until I heard of the *Playboy* translation that I brought it forward to make a kind of framework. Thereafter, whether delivered in Europe or America, the lecture had its present shape. But right from its inception, as a seminar at University College London in the early sixties, the solid substance remained the same. And, despite the date, was motivated neither by Women's Lib. nor the Permissive Society, but by my insistence on alerting our students to methodological problems arising from attempts to psychoanalyse the dead. From the kind of programme he'd persuaded me to engage in my splendid BBC producer rightly removed that intellectual muscle. One of these days I may restore it.   [E.M.W.]

Sexual Attitudes in Goethe's Life and Works
Elizabeth M. Wilkinson

In December 1968 Goethe finally made it! He made it into *Playboy Magazine*; and with a verse rendering of a narrative poem entitled 'The Diary' written when he was gone sixty. A poem long omitted from editions of his works or relegated to Notes and Appendices at the back; a poem recently described by a German professor in a history of German lyric poetry as 'lascivious' and 'obscene'. It is a poem about a sudden and totally unexpected onset of sexual impotence in a married male whose sexual performance has hitherto, as we are explicitly given to understand, been more than adequate. I am not a regular reader of *Playboy* myself. So I was unaware of Goethe's *succès d'estime* — or should it be *succès de scandale?* — until my attention was drawn to it by a male member of my audience in an American University. And I was hugely disappointed. For, having recently read a profile of P.G. Wodehouse by Philip Norman in *The Sunday Times* (Colour Magazine, 20 July 1969), in which he confessed to a strong distaste for the way his stories *looked* when they appeared in *Playboy* — 'half the page', as he put it, 'being devoted to a naked girl, and only a bit to your own story' — my expectations had run high. Poor Goethe, however, had to make do with two silhouettes, fully clothed in eighteenth-century style.

The translation of this 'Ribald Classic', as the *Playboy* version is sub-titled, is racy, rumbustious — and misleadingly inaccurate. It evades all the problems raised by Goethe's exploration of the modes of love and sexual morality in this rueful account of the recalcitrant antics of a man's 'nobler part'. To begin with, it omits the Latin motto with which he prefaced it, a motto taken from an elegy by Tibullus: 'I had another woman in my arms, but as I was about to take my pleasure Venus reminded me of my lady and deserted me' — thereby obscuring the tradition Goethe was working in, but at the same time modifying. It entirely distorts, presumably in the interests of ribaldry, or out of deference to our permissive society, not only the 'message' of Goethe's poem but also the ironic manner of his play on the classical tradition of didactic conclusions. For what Goethe actually wrote in his final stanza was this: 'And since, after all, every type of poetry is supposed to improve us [an obvious allusion to Horace's *delectare et prodesse*], I too will tread so popular a path, and gladly confess the import of my verses. Of course', he goes on, 'we slip and stumble on life's way. And yet, in this crazy world, two things can avail us much in our affairs: Duty, a great deal; how infinitely more, however, Love!'

> Sehr viel die Pflicht, unendlich mehr
> die Liebe!

What the *Playboy* translator makes of this is as follows:

> Look, it's a crazy world. We slip and stumble,
> But two things, Love and Duty, keep us going.
> I couldn't rightly call them hand in glove.
> Duty? — who really needs it? Trust your Love.

So Duty gets dismissed — which makes Goethe far less complex than he was. But he is made far less sexually outspoken too. For this translator has recourse to a variety of euphemisms and circumlocutions for the male organ: 'my impudent hero'; 'my dragging actor'; 'my sturdy ploughboy' etc. Goethe by contrast is plain and straightforward, and uses the same term throughout: namely, the masculine of the Latin demonstrative pronoun, *iste*; i.e. 'that there', 'that person or thing of yours' — sometimes prefacing it by 'Meister', with evidently enjoyable exploitation of the ambiguous nuances of such an honorific title in the context of male genitals.

Now the *Playboy* version may, as the editors claim, be the first rendering of the poem into English verse. But it is not the first translation into English. And when David Luke included it in the Goethe volume of *Penguin Poets* in 1964 he was faced with a very different, a very ticklish, problem indeed. His assignment for that bilingual series was to stick as close to the original as possible (hence prose). He had, therefore, to find an appropriate equivalent for Goethe's *Iste* — and stick to it throughout. If I now say that in following D.H. Lawrence and plumping for 'John Thomas', I doubt he hit upon the right one, I'm not suggesting I could have done any better. I'm raising the point only in order to look more closely at the linguistic and cultural texture of 'Das Tagebuch'. In the first place, Lawrence had no use at all for Goethe. In a letter to Huxley of 27 March 1928 he classed him among 'the grand perverts':

> Dear Aldous . . .
> . . . your idea of the grand perverts is excellent. You might begin with a Roman — and go on to St. Francis — Michael Angelo and Leonardo — Goethe or Kant — Jean-Jacques Rousseau or Louis Quatorze. Byron — Baudelaire — Wilde — Proust: they all did the same thing, or tried to: to kick off, or to intellectualize and so utterly falsify the phallic consciousness, which is the basic consciousness, and the thing we mean, in the best sense, by common sense. I think *Wilhelm Meister* is amazing as a book of peculiar immorality, the perversity of intellectu-alized sex, and the utter incapacity for any *development* of contact with any other human being, which is peculiarly bourgeois and Goethian. Goethe *began* millions of intimacies, and never got beyond the how-do-you-do stage, then fell off into his own boundless ego. He perverted himself into perfection and Godlikeness.

This list of 'grand perverts' is as fascinating as the notion of 'phallic consciousness' — a concept which might crudely, and in a way not altogether just to Lawrence, be paraphrased as: 'Do what the upstanding little man tells you and you can't go wrong'. For Lawrence *Wilhelm Meister* was an immoral book, not because of the immense variety of sexual attitudes it displays — heterosexual, homosexual, bisexual and incestuous — but because of the theme of 'Renunciation' which dominates its Second Part. And to another friend he had written over a decade earlier, 22 January 1916, explaining why: 'But whatever possessed you to quote me Goethe and "Reinheit"? . . . Purity lies in pure fulfilment, I should say. All suppression and abnegation seems to me dirty, unclean.' Sexuality was as important an element in the shaping of Goethe's life and work as in Lawrence's. But it's a very different kind of sexual consciousness.

But even if we reject 'John Thomas' we cannot simply retain the word *iste*, or any vernacular equivalent, until we know whether in using it Goethe was having recourse to the Latin as euphemism, or as a term current in the student slang of his own day — or whether in making it 'Meister Iste' he had quite other associations, maybe even legal, in mind. And this we do *not* know. What we do know is that he was much exercised in his own mind about the implications for a poet of the discrepancy between medico-anatomical terms, derived from Greek or Latin, and their sexual equivalents in the Vulgar tongue. In lines he himself excluded from his *Roman Elegies* he addresses a despairing plea to the classical god of fertility, Priapus, usually depicted with an outsize phallus. 'Give me, O Priapus', he cries, 'some other word for "tail". For, being German, I'm indeed sorely plagued as a poet. In Greek I could call you *phallus* — that falls splendid upon the ear. And in Latin *mentula* is not such a bad word either.' But then — with one of those 'etymological fantasies' in which Coleridge was so fond of indulging — he continues: '*Mentula* must, I suppose, come from *mens*' [isn't it rather the diminutive of *mentum* — 'the chin', including 'the beard' — i.e. a projection to the front?]. 'The tail, by contrast', he concludes, 'is something that comes from behind. And going in the back way is something I've never really enjoyed.' The last four of the seven-letter word *Schwanz* are still decorously replaced in German editions by dots:

> *Mentula* käme von *mens*, der Sch.... ist etwas
> > von hinten
> Und nach hinten war mir niemals ein froher
> > Genuss.

A corrective to this categorical statement later on! My point for the moment is the way in which sex is here made into such a comfortable bed companion with classical philology; as much integrated with civilized complexity as Lawrence's 'phallic con-sciousness' is set up against it.

Now not having had the pleasure or privilege of living with the great man — this is something I greatly look forward to in the after-life or in my next incarnation — Goethe's own sexual behaviour is something of which I have no first-hand knowledge. *Nor* any direct second-hand knowledge either! For despite his vast output of letters, conversations and diaries, his sexual prowess is something about which Goethe was reticent. All has to be inferred. And in this respect his biographers, including a couple of psychoanalysts, are in precisely the same position as myself. For the age of historiographical innocence is long past when a biographer could, with naive confidence follow the great Ranke's injunction and try to tell it like it was — 'wie es eigentlich gewesen'. And the case of, say, the Boston Strangler might be enough to put anyone off becoming an historian, or for that matter a psychologist, and trying to draw any such inferences. For the computerized 'profile' constructed from the evidence available while the police were still on the search was of a man who was the son of a domineering mother whom he hated, and whose sexual interest in women was therefore repressed and warped. What emerged when he was finally apprehended was that he was the favourite son of a warm-hearted mother to whom he was devoted, and that his sexual potency was phenomenal.

In the case of poets, the evidence from both poetic and non-poetic documentation is of course peculiarly complicated. Take the following observation: 'Pederasty is as old as humanity, and can thus be said to be within Nature although it is at the same time against nature.' If Goethe says this, in an authentically reported conversation at the age of eighty, we ought to know from his own extensive idiom just how to interpret it. It is the considered view of an old man about the place of homosexuality in human life. Maybe even in his own life. That is to say: pederasty does not serve Nature's prime purpose of propagating the species; but it is, nevertheless, an observable feature of animal, no less than human, behaviour. There is plenty of evidence in Goethe's letters, as in his poetry, that he was 'interested' in boys. But there is no evidence at all that he ever 'acted it out'. And as always when literature itself is used as evidence for diagnosing the nature of a poet, one cannot afford to neglect the complicating factors of tradition and style. Images may indeed be expressive of him as an individual. But he may also have been inspired to them through their traditional use by manifold predecessors. As Oscar Wilde pointed out: it is not always, with an artist, a case of feeling in search of a form; it may very well be a case of form in search of a feeling! May well be that, enamoured of a form such as the sonnet, the poet experiments with it — until he finds, caught up in its net, feelings of which he may have been unaware; feelings he may never have 'acted out'; situations which are an expression of wish-fulfilment rather than a record of events.

What irks me in many of Goethe's biographers is their reductive tendency where his love relations and sexual attitudes are concerned. For example: did he sometimes take flight from woman? Yes he did. But was it always he who took flight? No it wasn't? Sometimes *he* was rejected. This happened when he was a young man in Leipzig; and it happened when he was an old man of seventy in Marienbad — an experience which precipitated the greatest elegy in the German language. And were all his 'flights' for the same reason? Or did they involve the same quality of feeling? No, they didn't! Sometimes they involved guilt feelings — eloquently recorded by Goethe himself — and it is on these that biographers have lingered with such relish. Sometimes they were prompted by evident, and evidently unbearable, frustration: this was clearly the case with that married lady at the court of Weimar who is said by at least one psychoanalytical biographer to have had such therapeutic effect on him. According to this theory Goethe was, owing to his incestuous attachment to his sister, unable to achieve sexual consummation with a woman until the ripe old age of thirty-seven! What finally released him from the bonds of sibling attachment is said to be his ten-year-long, and profoundly passionate, relation with Charlotte von Stein. This, we are told, is to be regarded as an analogue of the psychoanalytic process: a release from sexual guilt feelings through transference of positive feelings on to the analyst, followed by the withdrawal of these, and their replacement by negative projections, symbolized in Goethe's case by his headlong flight from the Northern mists of Germany to the Southern sun and sensual expansiveness of Italy. I do not share this view. It is a mystery to me (though I owe much to both the theory and practice of psychoanalysis) how Charlotte von Stein's role in his life can seriously be compared to that of a psycho-analyst. I have yet to learn of a reputable analyst who could become so possessively involved, so bitterly lacking in joy at the alleged cure, so spiteful and malicious about her successor. It was enough to inten-sify Goethe's feelings of guilt instead of freeing him from them.

And sometimes his 'flights' were the result of genuine Renun-ciation — of *Entsagung*. Those who, like D.H. Lawrence, can see no difference between renunciation on the one hand, and repression or self-abnegation on the other, seem to me to know little about human life and living: about chance; or about the conjunctures and mismatched encounters arising from the fact that we live in time and space. It was *Entsagung* when Goethe, in his sixties, took flight — harshly maybe, for the pain obviously went too deep for words other than poetry — from the woman with whom, had they both been free, he might have made 'that marriage of true minds' which his romantically, or reductively, minded biographers would clearly have had him make. Yet Marianne von Willemer bore him no resentment. Oddly enough the only one of all his loves who did was precisely the one who was supposed to have had that profoundly therapeutic effect upon him! But what few, if any, of Goethe's biographers seem to understand, is the nature of marriage. And by 'marriage' I mean here an alliance, not necessarily sanctioned by either Church or State, but by those bonds of flesh which, though forged in sexual ecstasy, may survive when all passion is long spent: bonds strengthened by shared joys and sorrows; by the birth and sickness and death of children; bonds made unbreakable by memories, by gratitude and by mutual respect. Goethe married his mistress, Christiane Vulpius, when their eldest son was rising eighteen. He had defied the conventions and gossip of the little society in which he was not only Court poet, Ministerial Councillor, and intimate of the reigning Duke, but a figure — and increasingly so — of European eminence. He had defended their relationship, in verse and out of it, to his closest friends. It has to be a very reductive type of mind indeed that would try to explain away this late decision to 'marry the girl' by any one single motive. What *has* to be said — and may increasingly be understood by a freer generation — is that there was far more to this relationship than sexual attraction, a mother for his children, or an excellent cook-housekeeper. That if, on her death, he locked himself away and was heard sobbing 'You cannot leave me! You will not leave me' — this is not to be explained *away* by guilt feelings either. Until we reach a better understanding of Goethe's 'marriage' I don't think we can hope to understand either the variety, or the sum-total significance, of the sexual attitudes in his life.

And the same is true of his works. Far too much weight is placed on the interpretation of some single part snatched from the context of a larger whole. Take one of the Venetian Epigrams he

himself suppressed and which I promised earlier as a corrective to
one where he insisted that he'd never been partial to sodomy:
'Boys, of course, I've loved too. But girls I still loved far better.
When I've had my fill of her as girl, she can still serve me as boy.'
Out of context this may sound like the cynical confession of one
so late, and so thoroughly, released from sexual inhibition that
he's become a positive libertine. But consider its setting: em-
bedded in the profoundly sensual, sensitively aware, and richly
cultural texture of his *Roman Elegies* and *Venetian Epigrams*. Taken
in that context it reads quite differently. It becomes inseparable
from his playfully overt confirmation of all the serious talk which
generations of poets have taught us may go on in and among the
love-play of lovers: tapping out the hexameters of his verse on the
vertebrae of his sleeping beloved; or exploring the contours of her
body with 'seeing hand' and 'feeling eye'. Becomes inseparable
from his tender caring that she should not be ashamed of having
surrendered too promptly; or from his listening to the beat of the
foetal heart of their child as it grows in her belly. In this wider, and
intended, context the to some scabrous-sounding distich becomes
one of the many 'attitudes' (in the double sense of this word
intended by my own title) which lovers enjoy in the intimacy of
their love-play. It is as if he would say to her: 'Turn over now, love;
let's try it another way'.

Or take Edward Lockspeiser's interpretation of the last lines of
Goethe's *Faust* as they appear in Mahler's Eighth Symphony:

> Das Ewig-Weibliche
> Zieht uns hinan.

Some people, he wrote in *The Listener*, 27 July 1967, believe that
these two simple lines are the greatest in German poetry. Perhaps
they are, he conceded. But he went on:

> they are also sentimental lines. Who today can believe
> this notion? Womanhood does not draw us above,
> upward. We are more inclined today to think of an
> invading idea of womanhood, the huge mother-figure
> which envelops and oppresses us. Eternal womanhood is
> uplifting, says Goethe; but the voluptuous women of
> Baudelaire's poems — his prostitutes, mulattos, and
> Jewesses, also his serpents, cats, and corpses — have the
> opposite of an uplifting function. Here is the essential

difference between, on the one side Goethe, Beethoven, and Mahler — romanticists preoccupied with some rather 'lofty' ideal — and, on the other, Baudelaire, Wagner, and Freud, inquirers into the hidden workings of heart and mind. These were the artists — and I include Freud as an artist — primarily concerned with coming to terms with the forces of evil in human nature, with the concept of guilt, with sensuality.

And indeed we are now thus concerned. But all of this — and much more besides — is there in Goethe's *Faust* itself, if not in Mahler's setting of the final scenes. No one in his right mind would put Goethe in the same class as Baudelaire, Wagner or Edgar Allan Poe. But that's no reason at all for classifying him as a sentimental romanticist. We should have to look far in world literature for such a display of sexual perversions and obscenities as occur in his *Faust* — but, and this is the point, combined with such insight into the subterranean connections between sexuality and, say, religiosity; or with such understanding of the role the sinner has to play in the process of redemption. Just as we should have to look far indeed to find in one single cycle of poems such tenderly witty juxtapositions of hetero- and homosexual love, combined with such insight into the obscure, but undeniable, connections between homosexuality and pedagogy as we find in his *West-Eastern Divan*. Just as we should have to look far to find, before Freud, such consciously deliberate (as distinct from intuitive anticipatory) insights into the unconscious working of sexual fantasies in the consciously 'pure' mind of a pure woman as we do in Goethe's tremendous ballad 'Pariah' — a trilogy on the theme of the creation of a god for the pariahs of this world: for the outcasts and the despised. Or, as we do in his other great West-Eastern ballad 'Der Gott und die Bajadere', where there is an equally realistic, and ruthlessly presented, embodiment of the possible transmutation of Lust into Love. A ballad in which the 'God', having descended in order to experience all the suffering of the world, spends the night with a whore; a night in which she, having grace-fully and graciously offered him all the tricks of her trade, down to the ultimate in so-called perversion — finds that she loves him. That her Arts have been unexpectedly transformed into Nature, into 'second nature' as we say, through the ecstasy of Love.

It is with such subterranean interworkings of mind and body

that the poem I started with is really concerned. Sure it is, as
Playboy has it, 'a light, yet tender-hearted poem'. And sure it is
also, as Thomas Mann put it, 'eine kecke Moralität' (which sound,
as much as sense and associations, tempts me to render as 'a cocky
cautionary tale'). But it's more than either. If Thomas Mann's
judgment overstresses the 'moral lesson' drawn in its final stanza,
Playboy misses the *gravitas* evident in even the wittiest of Goethe's
'jests'. Perhaps the point of this poem comes out best if we read it
as a kind of answer to the *furore* created by the appearance of
Goethe's novel *Elective Affinities*, published six months before, in
the autumn of 1809. And indeed the poem may well have been
intended as an answer to the novel's reception. *Die Wahlver-*
wandtschaften is one of the great nineteenth-century novels on the
theme of adultery: of that kind of irresistible passion which can
brook no denial; which rides us, and overrides all other sanctions.
It was taken — hence the fuss — to be an attack by the Classical
Establishment on Romantic Attitudes: on their attitudes to free
love and marriage-partner swapping; on their obscuring of
distinctions between life and art; on their cults of the occult —
magnetism, water-divining, religiosity, and a whole lot of super-
stitions recently come back into vogue in our own time. It was
taken to be a defence of the institution of marriage. But the
curious thing is that the kind of marriage-counsellor figure —
appropriately and ambiguously named *Mittler*, which may signify
meddler as well as mediator — precipitates catastrophe every
time he opens his big trap: whether in defence of marriage or
to dilate upon the Seventh Commandment 'thou shalt not
commit adultery'. Another curious thing is that the solution of
divorce is proposed by the wife, who is unmistakably delineated
as the most reasonable character in the whole book. Yet a third
curious thing is that the most 'serenely' happy people in the book
(*heiter*, one of Goethe's favourite adjectives, is reserved for them)
are a third couple whom Goethe introduces as a foil to the other
two: a pair who have arrived at the amicable, and eminently
reasonable, solution of living six months a year with each other,
and six months with their respective spouses. But the ultimately
curious thing is that no adultery at all is committed. At least not in
civil law (canon law may be another matter). The famous
'adultery' scene takes place between the *married* couple, the
eminently reasonable wife and the anti-hero, that awful drip,

Eduard — each of whom is passionately involved with someone else. And during the whole of their love-play and final consummation — so intimately easy and familiar through long years of habit — their thoughts and fantasies are wholly engaged, not with each other, the partner present in the flesh, but with the absent belovèd. And — final and fearsome irony — the child born of this non-adulterous yet *how* 'adulterous' union, resembles neither of the physical partners present. It resembles both of the absent belovèds. A blatantly obvious symbol if you like. But a deliberately ironical — and ironically serious — one too.

We should go very wrong were we to conclude that Goethe is here suggesting that we can always control such fantasies during love-making even with our very own best belovèd. Or that, from some lofty moralistic standpoint, he's condemning them. What he is doing is rather to set up a fictional experiment. An experiment which may perhaps ultimately reveal something of the protean reality of love, but which, in the first instance, asks: What would happen if we were to take literally the scriptural text 'Whosoever looketh on a woman to lust after her hath committed adultery with her already in his heart'. Or, to put it in non-scriptural terms: What on earth would happen if the thoughts in our mind and the desires of our heart were always to find outward and visible expression in the world of so-called 'reality'? Who then would be judge? And by what criteria should he judge? Goethe is here raising the whole question of the influence of mind upon body, of the relation between flesh and spirit. And he is also raising the question of partial responses. Of failures in full reciprocity, whether sexual or not, between human beings.

And it is precisely such questions that he is following up in his light-hearted yet tender poem 'Das Tagebuch'. The narrator in this poem is a traveller who, absent from his wife on business (I always think of him as a commercial traveller because they're so exposed to such risks), keeps a diary for her. One evening the girl who serves him dinner at the inn readily agrees to come later to his bed. When she comes she tells him that he will be the first and — very important this — that she already loves him. The love-play proceeds, and is frankly described. And then, at the moment of entry, his organ refuses. This *Iste*, who has always been so hot and ready, and played the master, shrinks now like a schoolboy, 'all cooled off'. The girl, as yet sexually unawakened, and tired with her long day's work, falls asleep — wholly contented, apparently, by the preliminary love-play. He, by contrast, furious and ashamed at this sexual failure, fumes and frets . . . and then begins to recall how different it had been when he was courting his wife. How even at the altar — 'may God forgive me' (the near blasphemy is as bold as it is amusing) — that old 'Meister Iste' had riz up! He recalls the love-making of the bridal night, and countless other times thereafter when he had seized the opportunity in unlikely and unseemly places — in fields, on river banks, amid the reeds. And as he recalls all this, still lying beside the sleeping girl, quite involuntarily and quite contrarily, Master Iste does rise up, in all his customary splendour. He looks ruefully and tenderly upon her sweetness — then rises himself, to complete his diary for the day, concluding the record for his wife with the words that the 'ultimately important thing on *this* day' had been something that cannot be told in words. I for one am convinced that this 'ultimately important thing' was not just the confession of a foiled attempt at infidelity.

Sexual impotence, like cuckoldry, has traditionally been a theme for comedy and farce. And for some splendid poetry, not least in our own seventeenth century. But a student of mine, a girl, was once wiser about this than all those worldly-wise males who have, over the past twenty years, offered cynical comments after hearing me on the subject. The 'Love' implied by the final word of the poem, she pointed out, includes more than his love for his absent wife: it includes also a tender regard for the sleeping girl — for a girl who has been prepared to offer him not only sex but LOVE. This, and more than this, is true. We have here an exact reversal of the so-called adultery scene in *Elective Affinities*. There, in the novel, mind and body went their separate ways in a union which was — and still is, according to the standards of society — perfectly licit. Here, in the poem, a man fully prepared for a so-called illicit union, discovers — and discovers it through his most self-willed, but also 'nobler', part — that he would be taking his satisfaction, and temporarily maybe even giving some sort of satisfaction, by means of a physical manifestation not in the event called forth by the human being before him, however lovely and however desirable and desired, but by memories of, and sexual fidelity to, someone long and variously beloved. Does not Goethe here show a far more profound understanding of 'phallic consciousness' than Lawrence himself? An understanding of the strange workings of that most obviously intractable of human organs, and of the appetite — sexual appetite — which we have tended to think of, at least in the West, as an unlearned and unlearnable *instinct*? It seems to me that this poem, like so much else in Goethe's work, challenges us to reflect whether it will not be precisely after, and because of, full sexual permissiveness that we shall have to face up to the question of what sex really implies in terms of self-fulfilment, and self-limitation. Not least to the true nature of reciprocity. O.K. if both partners are agreed not only on 'the conditions' of the brief encounter, but on the quality of the involvement. But what happens when — and 'when' means pretty often — they aren't agreed? When the one expects something more than, and different from, the other? 'Duty' may then have to come in. And Goethe, unlike his *Playboy* translator, includes it in, even if in a subordinate capacity to 'Love'.

Reflections on Goethe's sexual attitudes may challenge us to revise many of our modern preconceptions. First, they may force us to question whether Freud's sublimation-theory of artistic creation was invariably right. Goethe's long life, which was a life of such evident human fulfilment, if not always of direct and obvious self-fulfilment, and which unlike, say, Wordsworth's was also, right up to the end, a life of sustained poetic creativity, certainly does not bear it out. It does not bear out either the inevitability of 'The Choice' expressed in the opening lines of Yeats's poem of that name:

> The intellect of man is forced to choose
> Perfection of the life or of the work.

Goethe was one who wasn't forced to make such a radical choice overall; though, like most of us, he was not exempt from having to choose in particular instances. Next, a consideration of his sexual attitudes challenges us to revise our preconceptions about the relation between unity and variety in this area of human experience: between norm and variations; between the moral and the psychological. Indeed, it invites us to reflect about a possibly different kind of reconciliation between the Many and the One from that which we in the West have, until recently, come to accept with all the force of a received idea. And last: the variety of sexual attitudes displayed so freely in his life and work, together with the sense of unity and continuity of which he was as deeply in need as most of us, forces us to reconsider that most basic and ubiquitous of all our preconceptions — or, as I call it, a heresy. Namely: whether spontaneity, spontaneous, self-fulfilling life, is *really* impaired by self-awareness, by taking thought. Clearly the kind of love Goethe had in mind in the last words of 'The Diary' is only to be achieved by a good deal of 'taking thought'.

The last thing Goethe would have wished us to do was to 'imitate' his way of life. When he spoke of his own life being an exemplary life, 'ein beispielhaftes Leben', what he clearly meant was that it was a typical example of the way of life that an ordinary man — 'l'homme moyen sensuel' — may be called upon to lead. Not an ascetic's life. Not a mystic's life. Not a recluse's life. And not just a poet's life either. But a life having the attributes of what André Gide was to call 'une banalité supérieure' (not of course to be rendered as 'a snooty sort of banality', but as 'banality raised to a higher power': — Gide was thinking of *gesteigert*, a word Goethe turned into a technical term in his scientific writings). What Goethe can certainly tell us something about — through his non-conformism, through the profusion and variety of sexual attitudes in both life and works — is how a man (or woman) may manage to live a life that is sacramental without benefit of sacraments. How to find meaning and value in a world where traditional forms and values were, even then, beginning to lose their hold, and had already ceased to provide the supporting framework they'd provided in the past. And he shows us that the one value we cannot dispense with is respect for wholeness: the wholeness in ourselves; the wholeness of others; the wholeness of the one and the many. Powerful urges such as sex can never be brought completely under control, can never be made predictable and unrecalcitrant. Nor can they ever be dealt with entirely by 'Duty' — though duty undoubtedly helps — unless we are to reduce the richness and variety of human response and human relationships, unless we are to maim and castrate ourselves. Such urges, like Meister Iste himself, 'lassen sich nicht befehlen, noch verachten': they are not to be commanded; but neither are they to be despised. They may in some measure be coped with by understanding. But, and this above all, they can only be truly accommodated by love:

> Sehr viel die Pflicht, unendlich mehr
> die Liebe!

Bibliography   R.B. Harrison

To conclude this volume of essays in English I have selected 71
books on Goethe (or including a discussion of Goethe) published
in English; 60 of these have appeared since the celebration in
1949 of the bicentenary of Goethe's birth, and over a third of
them in the last ten years. For full bibliographies the reader may
consult the Hamburger Ausgabe of *Goethes Werke*, a revised
edition of which has been published in 1981 (Munich, C.H. Beck)
and 1982 (Munich, Deutscher Taschenbuch Verlag); for a list of
translations of Goethe's works the reader should consult *Johann
Wolfgang von Goethe (1749-1832). Catalogue by Brian A. Rowley of an
Exhibition to mark the 150th Anniversary of Goethe's death on 22 March
1832,* Goethe-Institut London in association with John Calder
(Publishers) Ltd., 1982, pp. 66-69; and for a full appraisal of
Goethe's life and works the article by Elizabeth M. Wilkinson in
the *Encyclopaedia Britannica,* 1962, and recurrently brought up to
date.

Arber, Agnes, *Goethe's Botany. The Metamorphosis of Plants (1790) and Tobler's
    Ode to Nature (1782)*, Chronica Botanica, 10, Waltham, Mass., 1946
Atkins, Stuart, *Goethe's Faust. A Literary Analysis*, Cambridge, Mass., and
    London, Harvard University Press, 1958
Atkins, Stuart, *The Testament of Werther in Poetry and Drama*, Cambridge,
    Mass., Harvard University Press, 1949
Barnes, H.G., *Goethe's 'Die Wahlverwandtschaften'. A Literary Interpretation,*
    Oxford, Clarendon Press, 1967
Blackall, Eric A., *Goethe and the Novel,* Ithaca, N.Y., Cornell University
    Press, 1976

Bowman, Derek, *Life into Autobiography. A Study of Goethe's 'Dichtung und Wahrheit'*, Bern, Lang, 1971

Boyd, James, *Goethe's Iphigenie auf Tauris. An Interpretation and Critical Analysis*, Oxford, Blackwell, 1942

Boyd, James, *Goethe's Knowledge of English Literature*, Oxford, Clarendon Press, 1932

Brown, Jane K., *Goethe's Cyclical Narratives. 'Die Unterhaltungen deutscher Ausgewanderten' and 'Wilhelm Meisters Wanderjahre'*, Chapel Hill, University of North Carolina Press, 1975

Bruford, W.H., *Goethe's Faust I Scene by Scene. An Interpretation of Form and Content*, London, Macmillan, and New York, St Martin's Press, 1968

Bruford, W.H., *Culture and Society in Classical Weimar, 1775-1806*, London, Cambridge University Press, 1962

Bruford, W.H., *Theatre, Drama and Audience in Goethe's Germany*, London, Routledge and Kegan Paul, 1950

Burckhardt, Sigurd, *The Drama of Language. Essays on Goethe and Kleist*, Baltimore and London, Johns Hopkins Press, 1970

Butler, Elsie M., *Byron and Goethe. Analysis of a Passion,* London, Bowes and Bowes, 1956

Carlson, Marvin, *Goethe and the Weimar Theatre*, Ithaca, N.Y., Cornell University Press, 1978

Dieckmann, Liselotte, *Johann Wolfgang Goethe*, New York, Twayne, 1974

Fairley, Barker, *A Study of Goethe*, Oxford, Clarendon Press, 1947

Fairley, Barker, *Goethe's Faust. Six Essays*, Oxford, Clarendon Press, 1953

Fairley, Barker, *Goethe as Revealed in his Poetry*, London and Toronto, Dent, 1932

Farrelly, Daniel J., *Goethe and Inner Harmony. A Study of the 'schöne Seele' in the 'Apprenticeship of Wilhelm Meister'*, Shannon, Irish University Press, 1973

Friedenthal, Richard, *Goethe. His Life and Times*, London, Weidenfeld and Nicolson, 1965

Gearey, J., *Goethe's 'Faust'. The Making of Part I,* New Haven and London, Yale University Press, 1981

Gillies, Alexander, *Goethe's Faust. An Interpretation*, Oxford, Blackwell, 1957

Graham, Ilse, *Goethe. Portrait of the Artist*, Berlin and New York, de Gruyter, 1977

Gray, Ronald, *Poems of Goethe. A Selection with Introduction and Notes,* London, Cambridge University Press, 1966

Gray, Ronald, *Goethe. A Critical Introduction,* London, Cambridge University Press, 1967

Gray, Ronald, *Goethe the Alchemist. A Study of Alchemical Symbolism in Goethe's Literary and Scientific Works*, London, Cambridge University Press, 1952

Haile, H.G., *Artist in Chrysalis. A Biographical Study of Goethe in Italy*, Urbana, University of Illinois Press, 1973

Haile, H.G., *Invitation to Goethe's Faust*, University of Alabama Press, 1978

Hammer, Carl, *Goethe and Rousseau. Resonances of the Mind*, Lexington, University Press of Kentucky, 1973

Hatfield, Henry, *Goethe. A Critical Introduction*, Cambridge, Mass., Harvard University Press, 1964

Heller, Erich, *The Disinherited Mind*, Cambridge, Bowes and Bowes, 1952

Jantz, Harold, *Goethe's Faust as a Renaissance Man. Parallels and Prototypes*, Princeton University Press, 1951

Jantz, Harold, *The Form of Faust. The Work of Art and its Intrinsic Structures*, Baltimore and London, Johns Hopkins University Press, 1978

Jantz, Harold, *The Mothers in 'Faust'. The Myth of Time and Creativity*, Baltimore, Johns Hopkins University Press, 1969

Lamport, F.J., *A Student's Guide to Goethe*, London, Heinemann, 1971

Lange, Victor (ed.), *Goethe. A Collection of Critical Essays,* Englewood Cliffs, Prentice-Hall, 1968

Lee, Meredith, *Studies in Goethe's Lyric Cycles*, Chapel Hill, University of North Carolina Press, 1978

Leppmann, Wolfgang, *The German Image of Goethe*, Oxford, Clarendon Press, 1961

Lewes, G.H., *The Life and Works of Goethe*, London, Nutt, 1855 (now available in Everyman's Library, London, Dent, 1949)

Lukács, Georg, *Goethe and his Age*, London, Merlin Press, 1968

Mason, Eudo C., *Goethe's Faust. Its Genesis and Purport*, Berkeley and Los Angeles, University of California Press, 1967

Miller, R.D., *The Drama of Goethe*, Harrogate, Duchy Press, 1966

Miller, R.D., *'Wilhelm Meisters Lehrjahre'. An Interpretation*, Harrogate, Duchy Press, 1969

Needler, G.H., *Goethe and Scott*, Toronto, Oxford University Press, 1950

Nisbet, H.B., *Goethe and the Scientific Tradition*, Institute of Germanic Studies, University of London, 1972

Pascal, Roy, *The German Novel. Studies*, Manchester University Press, 1956

Pascal, Roy, *The German Sturm und Drang*, Manchester University Press, 1953

Peacock, Ronald, *Goethe's Major Plays*, Manchester University Press, 1959

Prudhoe, John, *The Theatre of Goethe and Schiller*, Oxford, Blackwell, 1973

Raphael, Alice, *Goethe and the Philosophers' Stone. Symbolical Patterns in 'The Parable' and the Second Part of 'Faust'*, London, Routledge and Kegan Paul, 1965

Reed, T.J., *The Classical Centre. Goethe and Weimar 1775-1832*, London, Croom Helm, and New York, Barnes and Noble, 1980

Reiss, H.S., *Goethe's Novels,* London, Macmillan, 1969

Richards, David B., *Goethe's Search for the Muse. Translation and Creativity*, Amsterdam, Benjamins, 1979

Roberts, David, *The Indirections of Desire. Hamlet in Goethe's 'Wilhelm Meister'*, Heidelberg, Winter, 1980

Robertson, J.G., *The Life and Works of Goethe 1749-1832*, London, Routledge, 1932

Robson-Scott, W.D., *The Younger Goethe and the Visual Arts,* Cambridge University Press, 1981

Rose, William (ed.), *Essays on Goethe,* London, Cassell, 1949

Simpson, James, *Matthew Arnold and Goethe,* London, Modern Humanities Research Association, 1979

Stahl, E.L., *Goethe: Iphigenie auf Tauris,* London, Edward Arnold, 1961

Steer, A.G., *Goethe's Science in the Structure of the 'Wanderjahre'*, Athens, Georgia University Press, 1979

Steer, A.G., *Goethe's Social Philosophy as Revealed in 'Campagne in Frankreich' and 'Belagerung von Mainz'*, Chapel Hill, University of North Carolina Press, 1955

Stewart, Walter K., *Time Structure in Drama. Goethe's Sturm und Drang Plays*, Amsterdam, Rodopi, 1978

Strich, Fritz, *Goethe and World Literature*, London, Routledge and Kegan Paul, 1949

Swales, Martin (ed.), *Goethe: Selected Poems,* London, Oxford University Press, 1975

Swales, Martin, *The German Bildungsroman from Wieland to Hesse*, Princeton University Press, 1978

Trevelyan, Humphry, *Goethe and the Greeks*, London, Cambridge University Press, 1941 (reissued with a Foreword by Hugh Lloyd-Jones, 1981)

Van Abbé, Derek, *Goethe. New Perspectives on a Writer and his Time*, London, Allen and Unwin, 1972

Wells, George A., *Goethe and the Development of Science, 1750-1900*, Alphen, Sijthoff and Noordhoff, 1978

White, Ann, *Names and Nomenclature in Goethe's 'Faust'*, Institute of Germanic Studies, University of London, 1980

Wilkinson, Elizabeth M., and Willoughby, L.A., *Goethe. Poet and Thinker*, London, Edward Arnold, 1962, 1970[2]

Index

Ann C. Weaver